I am blessed to know and see Pastor Dale Carver minister the word of Grace and son ship to all those who come under the influence of his gift and calling. Pastor Dale is a man according to God's own heart and has a heart to serve and equipped the body of Christ through all the nations of the world. I believe that his message in "The Real Man in the Mirror" is of vital importance to the body of Christ for our time because we cannot get people to their destiny if we first of all do not teach them about their IDENTITY in Christ. I strongly recommend that you read this book and begin to teach it's principle in your ministry and church. This is a must read for all of us.

Pastor Carlos Garcia
G.R.A.B the World Ministries Central America Director

I am a firm believer in the fact that there are answers awaiting you in the Presence of God. Any amount of time that you spend in His presence is never wasted. That is why this book "The Real Man in the Mirror", is so timely. Pastor Dale makes the wonderful truths of God's Word inviting and enriching. Far from taking a stodgy, hyper-academic approach, he presents powerful spiritual truths with great simplicity and clarity. He uses dynamic Bible principles that are extremely practical, relevant, and readily applicable. As I read thru it, I was encouraged, and challenged to act on these excellent spiritual insights. If you want your spiritual life raised to a new level, this book will be a wonderful catalyst for you, and a great asset for promoting maturity and growth in the Body of Christ.

Pastor Sittichai (Timothy)
Pastor Grace Gospel
Asia Director, G.R.A.B. the World Ministries

The Real
MAN IN THE MIRROR

CHRIST IN YOU, THE HOPE OF GLORY

DR. DALE CARVER

ISBN: 978-0-615-60796-2

Library Of Congress Control Number: 2012904082

Published in partnership:

GRAB the World Publishing
1497 W. 12th Street
Alma, Georgia
912-632-3744

Brikwoo Creative Group
Publishing Division
P.O. Box 1506
Trenton, Georgia
www.brikwoo.com

Cover Design & Page Layout: Brian Wooten

TABLE OF CONTENTS

DEDICATION

This book is dedicated to all my brothers and sisters who are being persecuted around the world for the gospel's sake. You are like Jesus. You are my heroes. To my friends from Myanmar who are in the Mae La Refugee Camp and others around the world that are deprived of basic physical liberties. Fences may keep you inside, but it cannot keep the Holy Spirit out. Keep the faith!

ACKNOWLEDGMENTS

I would first like to thank God for my wife and children. Family is the backbone of our society and I am blessed to have a very strong back. I love you! Thanks also to the members of First Community Church for allowing me to be me. You all are the greatest. I would especially want to thank Monica Richardson for her attention to detail and for always being ready to help in whatever role is needed. Special thanks go to all our covenant partners that finance and pray for all of our mission projects around the world. Thanks to my best friend in the ministry, Bishop Marlon Williamson. God sent me to Kenya to meet you. Words cannot express what being in relationship with you and your people has meant to our ministry. Thanks to my Pastor, Dr. Paul Harthern, who always has an encouraging word and who is full of wisdom. Pastor Paul and Mrs. Alvis are truly ambassadors of heaven. Thanks to Bishop David Huskins whose preaching and example always inspires me to reach for the heavens. Thanks to everyone for impacting and contributing to my life – you are all so special to me!

FOREWORD

As I ponder a trip that I took many years ago to be part of a pastor's training conference in Kenya Africa, I am so thankful that God was sovereignly working His plan to connect me with such a man as Dr. Dale Carver. I had no idea that this covenant relationship was about to begin.

Revelation 1:9 I John, who also am your brother, and companion in tribulation, and in the kingdom and patience of Jesus Christ...

I have found a brother and a companion in the kingdom in this man. Dr. Dale Carver is among a rare group of men that I call MEN OF GOD. He is not just a man preaching about God. He is a chosen vessel with an apostolic mantle on his life. He is a Man OF God.

When I try to think of words to describe him, I think of things like compassionate, passionate, faithful, wise, committed, honorable, real and much more.

As the years have passed and after traveling and ministering together in many places, one thing I have witnessed is that wherever Dr. Dale Carver ministers, Jesus is revealed and the works that He did, he does. The people he touches know that Jesus has been in the midst of them. People know that this man has been with Jesus.

The world is hungry and thirsty for present truth. The broken cisterns of man's religion have left many disappointed and unsatisfied. The world is desperately looking for hope. In this book, Dr. Dale Carver unveils the mystery that many are searching for; Christ In You, the hope of glory.

As you read the following pages, I pray that you will get a true revelation of the real man in the mirror. I pray that you will behold the glory of God when you see your true identity. I am convinced that we become what we behold. What you see is a matter of how you see the image. The scriptures declare that we are changed by the Spirit from glory to glory. We are changed in to the SAME image we behold. When you look in a mirror, you will see YOUR OWN face. If you can grasp the message of this book, you will never see yourself the same again.

Bishop Marlon Williamson
Word of Life Ministry
Fort Payne, Alabama

The primary declaration of Christianity is not "This do!"
but "This Happened!"
– Evelyn Underhill

Sovereign grace can make strangers into sons.
– C.H. Spurgeon

The God-image in man was not destroyed by the Fall but
was only damaged and corrupted ('deformed'), and can be
restored through God's grace.
– C.G. Jung

But we speak the wisdom of God in a mystery even the
hidden wisdom, which God ordained before the world unto
our glory. Which none of the princes of this world knew:
for had they known it, they would not have crucified the Lord
of glory.
1 Corinthians 2:7-8

INTRODUCTION

God created man in His Image and in His likeness. The correct image of man was taken from him in the fall of Adam. Death was passed to all man because of Adam's disobedience. Not only was death passed down but a faulty picture of man and his purpose was, too. The original mandate of man found in Genesis 1:27-28 was to be fruitful, multiply, replenish, subdue the earth, and to have dominion. Just because Adam fell does not mean that God changed His mind about who man was and the purpose in which he was created. Jesus came to seek and saved "that" which was lost. "That" which was lost was the whole purpose of man, the image in which he was created, and the relationship man had with Father God. Jesus has restored back to God "that" which was lost. Revelation of our true image is so needed in the body of Christ in order for us to grow up in Him and be the light that the world desires to see.

The greatest thing that ever has happened on Earth was a little over two thousand years ago just outside the city of Jerusalem. Jesus, the Savior, Lord, and King were crucified on an old rugged cross. Jesus, who took on a form of a servant, and was made in the likeness of men: And being found in fashion as a man, he humbled Himself, and became obedient unto death, even the death of the cross (Ph2:5-9). Isaiah prophesied in Isaiah 52:14 that his visage (his appearance) was marred more than any man. Why? So any man could regain his proper image. He became a son of man so that you could become a son of God. Jesus laid down His life in order that you could pick up His life. He came to restore your image back to God. A positive self-image is a crucial thing for anyone to have in order to attain success. In fact, I would dare say that you will not be successful without one.

Philemon 6, That the communication of thy faith may become effectual by the acknowledging of every good thing which is in you in Christ Jesus.

You were created to have success and to fulfill your purpose. In fact, you were created to be like Jesus. Jesus is the only example of a perfect man. You are now in Him. He is now in you. You need to start acknowledging every good thing that is in you. Your image needs to improve first in your own mind. God sees you through the sacrifice of Calvary. He sees you in Christ, and He sees Christ in you, which the Bible declares is the hope of glory *(Co1:27)*. A false humility will never get you anywhere. True humility is looking at what God did for you and knowing that you had absolutely nothing to do with it. It is all by the unmerited grace of God. God loves you and wants you to know how much He loves you. He sings over us. As I was writing this, the old Joe Cocker love song, "You Are So Beautiful," has been sounding out in my spirit. It is a song that we could also sing to God, but more importantly, I believe it is a song that He sings over us. To Him, we are so beautiful. We are everything He has ever hoped for. We are everything He needs. He desires a real relationship with His children. From the beginning of creation, that is all He has ever wanted.

A man with a sin conscience will never fully approach God. Jesus took away that sin man and has made you the righteousness of

God. Now you can approach God anytime. You can enter the throne room of grace boldly and talk with your heavenly Father. By His blood and with His name, we can enjoy the rights and privileges of being His son. You can walk with God just like Adam did before the great fall. Jesus has transformed you, making you incredibly beautiful.

The primary purposes behind this book are to get you to see the real man in the mirror, and to restore a right understanding of your true identity. This will reveal what you can do and what you are called to do while you are on the earth. To me, this has been the greatest revelation that I have ever received. I guess I needed it worse than most. Because I was brought up in a traditional Pentecostal home (although I do thank God for my heritage) I felt that we worshipped a God that was "way up there somewhere." In fact, my understanding was that He was too holy to approach, and certainly unable to become friends with. In my mind, one day after this life, maybe if I died right with Jesus, just maybe, I could go to heaven. Jesus taught us to pray "thy will be done in earth as it is heaven." *(Matthew 6:10)* God is concerned about you and this earth. God is not through with this earth. Much of the religious world puts all the promises off until some future time, but the Lord has shown me to live "in the now." Eternity is a sure thing, and while I do thank God for the future, our now can also be glorious. "Now" faith is... *(Hebrews 11:1)*

I see that all revelation, all illumination, everything that God had in Christ was to be brought forth into perfect light that we might be able to live the same, produce the same, and be in every activity sons of God with power. We must not limit the Holy One. And we must clearly see that God brought us forth to make us supernatural; that we might be changed all the time on the line of the supernatural; that we may every day live so in the Spirit, that all of the revelations of God are just like a canvas thrown before our eyes, on which we see clearly step by step all the divine will of God.

– Smith Wigglesworth

Obedience brings possession. Possession brings Christlikeness. Christlikeness brings power.

– Smith Wigglesworth

Never lose an opportunity of seeing anything beautiful; for beauty is God's handwriting.

– Ralph Waldo Emerson

Chapter One
BEAUTIFUL ONE

"You are so beautiful!" I told a little girl while fellowshipping in the social hall of a Tennessee church that I had just finished ministering in. When I asked her age, she answered "nine." I said jokingly, "How did you get so pretty in just nine years? It took me forty nine years to get ME this pretty." She responded by giving me such a beautiful smile. Children are so beautiful in their innocence. The body of Christ is so beautiful, too. We have been made righteous and holy by the precious blood of Jesus. It occurred to me that, just like the conversation with the little girl, it could be true with our heavenly Father and all of His children. To Him even with all of our natural faults and short comings, we are so beautiful.

Ephesians 2:10, For we are His workmanship (His masterpiece), created in Christ Jesus unto good works, which God hath ordained that we should walk in them.

Romans 8:28-33, And we know that all things work together for good to them that love God, to them who are called according to His purpose. For whom He did foreknow, He also did predestinate to be conformed to the image of His Son, that He might be the firstborn of many brethren. Moreover whom He did predestinate, them He also called: and whom he called, them He also justified: and whom He justified, them He also glorified (new creation in all of His beauty). What shall we then say to these things? If God be for

THE REAL MAN IN THE MIRROR

us, who can be against us? He that spared not His own Son, but delivered him up for us all, how shall He not with Him also freely give us all things? Who shall lay anything to the charge of God's elect? It is God that justifies.

These scriptures will be my launching pad to explain how beautiful you are right now in the eyes of God. Remember that God sees the end from the beginning and yes, He is still working on us. However, 1 Peter 1:9 tells us to receive the end of our faith. Hebrews 11:1 defines faith as the substance of things hoped for, the evidence of things not seen. Just because you cannot see the end of your faith does not mean that your heavenly Father does not see. Romans 8:29 reminds us that we have a destiny! Our destiny is not a geographical location. I used to think that it was. Many years ago, I dreamed that I was preaching in China to a large population of Chinese. Because of this, I mistakenly thought for a long time that, if I could just preach in China, then I would be at my destiny. However, that reasoning is so wrong. Our destiny is not a geographical location, but a Person – Jesus Christ.

YOUR DESTINY IS A PERSON

We were predestined to be like Jesus (Romans 8:29). We are His representatives here on earth. He is the firstborn of many brethren *(Romans 8:29)*. 1 John 4:17 declares because as He is, so are we in this world. That is such a powerful verse of scripture. As JESUS IS, so are we. Jesus said in Acts 1:8 that after the Holy Ghost has come upon us, we would be His witnesses. In John 14, he stated that we would do the works that He himself did and even greater works. Was He lying, or was it indeed possible to live like Jesus, walk like Jesus, talk like Jesus, be like Jesus? I want to emphasize that YOU are the only Jesus some people will ever see. It is Christ in you, the hope of glory *(Col1:27)*. Remember Romans 8:30 tells us "...them He justified, He has also glorified." Now we can begin to see the end from the beginning. The end is that we are to be like Christ, mature sons of the Most High God. The end is glorious, and we are to receive the end of our faith now. Romans 8:19 reveals that the whole earth is groaning, waiting on the manifestations of the sons of God. Please read the entire chapter of Romans 8. Not only is it my favorite chapter in the Bible, it is a chapter of the Spirit. The Spirit of God brought you to the Lord, and it is the same Spirit that will teach us and lead us to being more like the Lord Jesus. It was the Spirit that drove Jesus into the wilderness directly after His baptism. Jesus conquered every attack of the enemy and came out in the power of the Spirit. In our own wilderness experiences, we too can come out as Jesus did in the power of the Spirit. In everything that we go through, He will purify us and we shall come out shining like pure gold. Therefore, we win no matter what!

SILVER & GOLD
REDEMPTION AND DIVINITY

When gold or silver is being mined from the earth, even though it is very valuable, it is not all that beautiful. It does not come out of the earth fashioned like a ring or some other jewelry. There is not a polished shine on this raw material. It has not been through the process of being refined or purified. In this state, the silver or gold is not pure. There are other minerals and dirt attached to it. Although, it is still very valuable in its current condition, it is not useful until it has been processed or refined. There are years of dirt and other things that must be removed from it to be at its optimum value. You also are so valuable to God. Like the gold or silver there must be a refining, we have been mined from the earth. According to where we were mined from (background and experiences), indicates how much dirt and junk there is, and how long we must be in the fire of purification. Although I had so much dirt and junk attached to me, God still loved me the same on that day that I was mined as He does today. In fact, I was just as much saved then as I am now. But He had to begin the process of cleaning me up and burning some stuff off of me. He is still removing "junk". I had a lot of nasty and ugly religion attached (along with other things). Please do not misunderstand me. I am a "finished work" grace preacher and you are precious in His sight right now. However, He wants perfected praise from you and He wants you to be a vessel of honor that is sanctified and prepared for every good work *(2 Timothy 2:21)*. You have a divine purpose. Jesus has finished His work on Calvary, and now we must get started with our work. We are laborers together with God *(1 Corinthians 3:1-11)*. He wants us to continue to always be improving on ourselves to become all that God has intended us to be -- vessels of honor like Jesus. We are sons of God like Jesus. I say often that He (Jesus) is the big "S" while we are the little "s". He is the firstborn among many brethren. (Romans 8:29) Jesus is Lord of lords!

VESSEL OF HONOR

2 Timothy 2:19-21, nevertheless the foundation of God stands sure, having this seal. The Lord knows them that are His. And, let everyone that names the name of Christ depart from iniquity. But in a great house there are not only vessels of gold and of silver, but also wood and of earth; and some to honor and some to dishonor. If a man therefore purge himself from these, he shall be a vessel unto honor, sanctified, and meet for the master's use and prepared unto every good work.

Malachi 3:1-4, Behold, I will send my messenger, and he shall prepare the way before me: and the Lord, whom you seek, shall suddenly come to His temple (you are the temple of the living God), even the messenger of the covenant, whom you delight in: behold, he shall come, saith the Lord of hosts. But who may abide the day of His coming? And who shall stand when He appeareth? For He is like a refiner's fire, and like fuller's soap: And He shall sit as a refiner and purifier of silver: and He shall purify the sons of Levi, and purge them as gold and silver, that they may offer unto the Lord and offering in righteousness. Then shall the offering of Judah and Jerusalem be pleasant unto the Lord.

Offerings have always been important to the Lord. If we were to go back to Genesis to find the first recorded mention of man's offering, we would see that God accepted one, but rejected the other. Can we conclude that God still accepts and rejects an offering? I certainly want my offerings to be acceptable to Him. In the eleventh chapter of Hebrews, we are told that "Abel offered his offering by faith" (Hebrews 11:4) But without faith it is impossible to please the Lord (Hebrews 11:6). So we must decide that our offerings must be done in faith. This faith is in what Jesus did though, not what we are doing. What hinders faith many times is a sin consciousness. We need to transform this into a righteous conscience. This comes by knowing what Jesus did for you on Calvary and the power of His shed blood. "What can wash away my sins? Nothing but the blood. What can make me whole again? Nothing but the blood." The blood has already cleansed us. However, when we commit sin or have a sin conscience, then it will hinder our faith. Faith hindered or you could say doubt manifested could hinder your offering to be accepted by the Lord. Therefore, we must rid ourselves of this sin conscience and the carnal Adamic nature. We must bury the first Adam and then marry the last Adam: Christ.

It is the grace of God that teaches me to deny ungodliness *(Titus 2:11-12)*. What rules and the Law could not do, the grace of God has done. Grace has made me holy. We are saved by grace. I like what my friend Dr. Lynn Hiles says, "It is not about rules that you can keep, but about a life that can keep you." What I am referring to is being like Jesus, a vessel of honor, a mature son in the kingdom of God fulfilling your purpose on planet Earth. I want to be like Jesus, and I hope that you do, too. This is our destiny, but in order to fulfill our purpose, we must put on Christ and bury the old man – once and for all.

Jesus is King of kings and Lord of lords. You are among the kings and lords that He is over. You are the silver that is redeemed. You are the gold that needs to be refined.

Malachi chapter 3 verse 2 says that "He is like a refiner's fire and fullers' soap." Soap and fire will clean and purify, but He will sit as a refiner. When Jesus comes, He comes to purify. In other words, instead of praying for deliverance from a situation or circumstance that is uncomfortable to be in, we may need to realize that our Deliverer may be the One (Refiner) that has turned up the heat. It is our sweet Jesus that said in Luke 12:49 that "He has come to send fire upon the earth." The fire that will burn up the earth is not referring to end times, but instead, burning the earth away from you so that you will shine like pure gold. Gold speaks of divinity.

A TEST = A TESTIMONY

2 Peter1:4 affirm that you might be made partakers of the divine nature. God may allow you to get angry so that you learn to deal with your own anger problem. God will allow obstacles in your way so you can learn to overcome the obstacles. He wants us to learn how to use the authority that He has given to overcome these problems. Until we learn how to speak to the mountain that is in front of us and command it to move. God will allow resistance to enable us to become stronger. God will even permit you to go through some things so you will GO THROUGH. God may let you endure pain in order to learn how to love through this pain, empathize, and have compassion for others who are also hurting. Jesus Himself learned obedience by the things He suffered (Hebrews 5:8). Do you think David would have ever become king without Goliath? It was Goliath that propelled him into his future and prepared him to become king. At the end of the day, "all things work together for the good of those that love the Lord and are called according to His purpose *(Romans 8:28)*." We win no matter what!

We have been predestined to be like Jesus. If you will allow God to have His perfect work, you will come out shining like pure gold and silver that has been refined. Silver, which speaks of redemption, is not pure until the silversmith can see His image in the silver. He must see His reflection, or He is not satisfied. God wants to see His image in the earth. You were created in His image and in His likeness. When God made man, He formed man out of the earth. You have the fingerprints of God all over you. God breathed into Adam the breath of life. If it takes more fire and more heat to bring it out in me, then so be it. If I have to pass another test, "bring it on." There is no weapon formed against me that shall prosper. Jesus has promised that He would never leave me nor forsake me *(Hebrews 13:5)*. He assured me "that all things work together for my good *(Romans 8:28)*." I am ready to be more like my Lord! Remember, everything that we go through works to fulfill God's plan for us and that is to have us become more like the Lord Jesus Christ. We win – no matter what!

You cannot have a testimony without a test. You cannot overcome without an obstacle. You cannot be a victor without a battle. The battle is not just the devil, but it is with our own mind and thoughts. Through the years we have fortified wrong beliefs (established strongholds) about ourselves with religious teachings. The weapons of our warfare are not carnal but are mighty through God for the pulling down of strongholds, casting out imaginations, and taking every thought captive *(2 Corinthians 10:4-5)*. Our mind must be renewed. When your traditions and beliefs contradict the truth of God's Word, you must go with the Word of God. All traditions and beliefs must bow the knee to truth. The Word of God has treasures that we are to search out and study to show ourselves approved. This is crucial if we are to become a workman that is not ashamed.

We can get a better image of who we truly are and how we are to live in the Word of God. The Word of God is a mirror.

God is longing for us to come into such a fruitful position as the sons of God, with the marks of heaven upon us, His divinity bursting through our humanity, so that He can express Himself through our lips of clay. God can take clay lips, weak humanity, and make an oracle for Himself. He can take our frail human nature and by His divine power wash our hearts whiter than snow and make our bodies His Holy temple.
— Smith Wigglesworth

I believe that God, the Holy Ghost, wants to bring us into line with such perfection of beatitude, of beauty, that we shall say, "Lord, Lord, though you slay me, yet will I trust you." When the hand of God is upon you and the clay is fresh in the Potter's hands, the vessel will be made perfect as you are pliable. Only melted gold is minted; only moistened clay is molded; only soften wax receives the seal; only broken, contrite hearts receive the mark as the Potter turns us on His wheel – shaped and burnt to take and keep the mark, the mold, the stamp of God's pure gold.
— Smith Wigglesworth

Chapter Two
YOU LOOK BETTER THAN YOU THINK!

Have you ever met a really beautiful person with low or little self-esteem? Some people do not seem to realize just how beautiful they are. Each Sunday before I preach to my local church, I will instruct everyone to go to several people and shake hands with each other, and tell them how beautiful they are in the Lord. The Bride of Christ is so beautiful. You are so beautiful. You do not have a blemish, you are without spot. We just need faith to see who and what we really are, the way God created us to be. God sees our potential, not our problems. God sees the end from the beginning.

I have preached a sermon using a peach as an illustration. I ask the congregation what they see, and they will answer, "A peach or fruit." Then I ask them what they think God sees? Remember, He sees the end from the beginning. His visual images are entirely different from ours. He sees peach orchards. He sees jobs for people picking and processing the peaches. He even sees cooks cooking peach cobblers and baking peach pastries. He even sees me enjoying the cobbler. He views ships being loaded with peaches to go around the world and He sees many other things all from that one peach. Do you know why? It is because the peach has inside a very powerful substance. The peach has a seed, and there is nothing more powerful than a seed. You also have a Seed inside of you. God sowed a Son, so He could reap a family. God sees the

Seed! There is more in you than you can possibly imagine!

Proverbs 25:2-5, It is the glory of God to conceal a thing: but the honor of kings is to search out a matter. The heaven for height, and the earth for depth, and the heart of kings is unsearchable. Take away the dross from the silver, and there shall come forth a vessel for the finer. Take away the wicked from before the king, and his throne shall be established in righteousness.

We must remember that our mind is what will attempt to condemn us, but He is greater than our minds. What He did on Calvary is greater than anything we will ever be able to do. When Christ died on the cross, He died not only for you, but He died as "you". He took your place. It is appointed man once to die and after that the judgment. Jesus prophesized "if I be lifted up, I will draw all men unto me." In some churches today many worship leaders still use that verse as a worship verse to get people to praise Him more fervently. That is a great misinterpretation because Jesus was talking about being lifted up on the cross. According to this scripture, while He was lifted up, you and I were drawn to Him. He paid the complete sin -debt for the whole human race – your sins, my sins, and all of humanities. Judgment went upon Jesus – not on us!

Because the anger and wrath of God went upon Jesus instead of us, we must realize that God is not angry with us now. Your sin debt was fully paid. I heard Bishop David Huskins once say something so liberating for those that were brought up in a very religious atmosphere like I was and feel that they cannot live up to God's standard. He emphatically told the congregation, "What God did in Christ at Calvary is greater than anything you can ever do in Adam." We all need to fully understand what happened when Jesus died. Behold the Lamb of God which takes away the sin of the world!

God has now put His seed in us. He has crowned us with glory. He has given us everything we need to live this resurrected life. Greater is He that is in us than he that is in the world *(1John4:4)*. We can overcome because He has already overcome. We are married to Jesus now. Not one day, way up yonder in the sweet by and by but right now, we are the Bride of Christ. We are the beautiful bride that is without spot or blemish. If we are not married to Him, then it would be unlawful for us to be intimate with Him. But he longs for an intimate relationship with us. It would also be unlawful for us to produce anything from that relationship. But Jesus has called us to be fruitful and to produce. He wants us to multiply and go around the world with the gospel. Because we have accepted Jesus, we are one with Him – right now! We need to stop procrastinating our blessings until the future, and start living in the now. Again, I thank God for our future. It will be glorious, but our "now" means we have divine purpose on earth. Why are we still gazing into the heavens like the apostles in the first chapter of Acts? Let us get busy with bringing in the harvest. Now faith is… We need a breakthrough now. We need healings now. We need the manifestations of glory now. Now we need to evangelize the world. Jesus said, "Don't say three or four months and then comes harvest. Look on to the field. They are white unto harvest now. God is a present help. Today is the day of salvation. God will hear you now. You can receive your blessing now!

1Corinthians 6:17, But he that is joined to the Lord is one spirit.

We have the same spirit that raised Christ from the dead NOW dwelling in us. Right now, the same Holy Spirit that raised Christ from the dead is inside of your body. You are the temple of the Holy Spirit *(1Co3:16)*. The same Spirit that enabled Christ to perform miracles and baffle the scholars with His wisdom is inside of you. The same Spirit that anointed Jesus has anointed you. You have unction to function. You have been given much grace! God is with you at this very moment – live in the now.

JESUS ON THE INSIDE, JESUS ON THE OUTSIDE

The next three verses are so powerful, liberating, and instructional. Please read carefully.

2 Corinthians 4:7; 10-11, But we have this treasure in earthen vessels, that the excellency of the power may be of God and not of us. 10, Always bearing about the dying of the Lord Jesus, that the LIFE ALSO OF JESUS MIGHT BE MADE MANIFEST IN OUR BODY. 11, For we which live are always delivered unto death for Jesus' sake, THAT THE LIFE ALSO OF JESUS MIGHT BE MADE MANIFEST IN OUR MORTAL FLESH.

Sometimes a preacher may repeat himself because he is naturally long-winded or he forgets that he said a certain thing. Most of the time he is repetitious, though, it is because he feels it is extremely important. He wants the hearer to fully comprehend what is being said. The great apostle Paul had to repeat himself in verses 10 and 11 because it was so important that it deserved reemphasis. All scripture is given by inspiration of the Holy Spirit. Paul did not write this to fill up space or because he was "wordy". He wrote this twice because it is crucial to our understanding of what type of life we are to live. It is our destiny and purpose to be like Jesus and to show the world Jesus. These verses are very plain and can be understood by anyone. WE ARE TO BE SHOWING THE WORLD JESUS. JESUS IS TO BE MANIFESTED FROM OUR BODY. It is not I that live, but it is Christ Jesus that lives in me. The life which I now live in the flesh, I live by the faith of the Son of God, who loved me, and gave Himself for me *(Galatians 2:20-21)*. We are predestined to be like Jesus *(Romans 8:29)*. So we can rejoice and truly be thankful in all things. Even in tough times, God is working all things together for our good that so we can live out our destiny and fulfill our purpose in showing the world Jesus. By doing this, we come out shining like pure gold.

1 Peter 1: 3-10, Blessed be the God and Father of our Lord Jesus Christ, which according to His abundant mercy hath begotten us again unto a lively hope by the resurrection of Jesus Christ from the dead, To an inheritance incorruptible, and undefiled, and that fades not away, reserved in heaven for you. Who are kept by the power of God through faith unto salvation ready to be revealed in the last time. Wherein you greatly rejoice, though now for a season, if need be, you are in heaviness through manifold temptations (trials): That the trial of your faith, being much precious than of gold that perishes, though it be tried with fire, might be found unto praise and honor and glory at the appearing of Jesus Christ: Whom having not seen, you love; in whom, though now you see Him not, yet believing, you rejoice with joy unspeakable and full of glory; Receiving the end of your faith, even the salvation of your souls. Of which salvation the prophets have enquired and searched diligently, who prophesied of the grace that should come upon you.

The trials of our faith are more precious than gold that perishes, though it is tried with fire. It is at this point (when we are facing the trials) that we must fully trust in our Lord. Proverbs commands us that we are to trust in the Lord with all of our heart and lean not unto our own understanding. Jesus our silversmith will not leave us in the fire for one micro-second longer than we need. We are His workmanship, His masterpiece *(Ephesians 2:10)*. We are His Bride. We are heirs of God and joint heirs with Christ *(Romans 8:17)*. God has our best interests in His heart. We must trust His plans for our lives and for the lives of others who we love and care for. Even when we do not understand what is going on around us, we must cling to the fact that He knows best. There is an old song that says something like this "when I cannot see His hand, I can trust His heart." We must always look to Jesus and depend on the leading of the Holy Spirit. God is in control. He loves us and sees the end from the beginning. We are being changed with every trial and test that comes our way.

2 Corithians 3:17-18, Now the Lord is that Spirit and where the Spirit of the Lord is, there is liberty. But we all, with open face beholding as in a glass (mirror) the glory of the Lord, are changed into the same image from glory to glory, even as by the Spirit of the Lord.

These are two of my favorite verses. It speaks of us looking in a mirror. A person looks in the mirror to see himself. The Bible or the Word of God is a mirror, and by reading it, we get a picture of what we are to look like. Remember, that we are to look like Jesus. Verse 18 tells us that as we look into the mirror, we are to behold the glory of the Lord. We are looking at ourselves because that is what we do with mirrors, but we need to be seeing the glory of the Lord. While we are beholding the glory of the Lord, something is happening. We are being changed into the same image from glory to glory. This is truly a work of the Spirit. The Spirit of the Lord is transforming us from glory to glory. We are going from faith to faith. Because we are maturing and being conformed to the image of His Son, our destiny is in reach. This is "mission possible," not "mission impossible." However, our perspective must be correct. We cannot have a "woe is me" attitude, or "I am just a sinner saved by grace." Some people even think of themselves as "a wretched worm." You were a sinner, you were saved by grace, but you are now a new creation, created in Christ Jesus. Can you see the glory? Paul said, "I should somewhat more boast of our authority" *(2Co.10:8)*. There is a metamorphosis (transformation) that is occurring *(see Romans 12:1-2)*. Just like the changes that take place for a caterpillar to become a butterfly, so are your changes. To me, there are not too many things uglier than a caterpillar or as beautiful as the butterfly after the transformation. You are gold and even more beautiful than the butterfly! Get ready for the change. Transformers are coming not in a theater near you, but all over the world. God's children are putting on His image and doing great exploits. Change, real change is on the way. You are being changed, so that you can change the world.

John 1:12, But as many as received Him, to them gave He power to become sons of God, even to them that believe on His name.

We are to live as sons of God on earth. Thy will be done on or in earth as it is in heaven. His will is for us to be like Jesus.

Philippians 2:5-6,13, and 15, Let this mind be in you, which was also in Christ Jesus: Who, being in the form of God, thought it not to be equal with God. 13, For it is God which works in you both to do will and to do His good pleasure. 15, That you may be blameless and harmless, the sons of God, without rebuke, in the midst of a crooked and perverse nation, among whom you shine as lights in the world.

It seems that some people want to become sons of God after death, but this verse is clear that we are to live as sons of God in the midst of a crooked and perverse nation. We are to let our light shine before men and show them the Way. Jesus is the Way, Truth, and Life *(John 14:6)*. The psalmist David wrote that "He prepares me a table in the presence of mine enemies." We often use this passage at funerals, but this psalm is for us living in the present world, too. He anoints my head with oil. My cup runs over. Goodness and mercy are following me all the days of my life. Praise God! I do not think I will have enemies on the other side. This psalm is for us here on earth. All scriptures are for us here.

Let the mind of Christ be in you, which was also in Christ Jesus: Who, being in the form of God, thought it not robbery to be equal with God: But made Himself of no reputation, and took upon Him the form of a servant *(Philipians 2:5-8)*.

Let's serve the world by showing them Jesus. Christ in you is the hope of glory *(Colossians1:27)*. If there is hope for a great awakening, a great revival, a great move of God, then it will come out of us, His body. Jesus is not going to manifest himself in thin air to preach to the millions that have not heard. He will come to and through His people. Can you imagine how the church could change the world for good if we simply got back to showing it Jesus?

We must put on Christ and let the purifying fire purge the earth and dross away from us so the divine nature stands out in us. David said again, I shall be satisfied when I awake with your likeness *(Ps17:15)*. David was a man after God's heart. He knew God's ways and He pursued them. He was definitely not a perfect man in the flesh, but he was the only one that God testified that "was after His heart." Could He say that about you? Are we after the heart of God? God wants to see His image in the earth. You were made in His image and in His likeness. He will not share His glory with "another," but you are not "another." You are so much like Him. You are His image and He has crowned you with glory *(Hebrews 2:7)*. He has called us to glory *(2Peter 1:3)*. He shall supply all of our needs according to His riches in glory *(Philippians 4:19)*. To them He predestined, He called: Whom He has called, them He has justified: and them He has justified, is them He has also glorified *(Romans 8:30)*. Let it sink in. You are the Temple of the Lord now and the Lord of Glory has crowned you. You are certainly not unclean or common.

Don't let the human mind interfere with the great plan of God. Submit yourself to God. May the divine likeness of Him who is the express image of the Father dwell in you richly, abounding through all, supplying every need, bringing you into a place where you know the hand of God is leading you from treasure to treasure, from grace to grace, from victory to victory, from glory to glory, by the Spirit of the Lord.
– Smith Wigglesworth

Man the failure, the sin-ruled, the Satan-dominated, held in bondage by the unseen forces of spiritual darkness, is to be recreated, made a New Creation, taken out of the family of Satan and "translated into the Kingdom of the Son of love," on legal grounds. This is the solution of the human problem: God giving His Nature, His Love, to fallen man. He is no longer a fallen man. He is a New Creation man united with Jesus Christ, the Head of the New Creation. He has "raised us up together with Christ' man.
– E.W Kenyon

Chapter Three

YOU ARE NOT COMMON

In Acts 10, God hears the prayers of a Gentile man and tells him to send for the Apostle Peter. Peter, at that time, is having a vision on a rooftop about all kinds of animals being let down into a sheet. The Lord speaks to Peter in the vision, telling him to rise up, slay the animals, and eat them. When Peter refuses and tells the Lord that he has never eaten any common or unclean animal, the voice speaks a second time and rebukes him saying, "WHAT GOD HAS CLEANED, YOU DO NOT CALL COMMON? (Verse 15)."

This is a very interesting passage of scripture to me. First of all, the vision represented not unclean animals, but the Gentiles. A Jew like Peter would never have gone into Cornelius' house without first having this vision. Gentiles were uncircumcised with no covenant rights and were considered unclean. God was doing a new thing by opening up the gospel to the whole world. God has always wanted a relationship with man – any man regardless of nation, tribe, or tongue. God was getting ready to share his message to the world by what He had done through His Son, Jesus. All of us could now have a relationship with Him. There is now neither male nor female, Jew or Greek. We are all one in Christ (Galatians 3:28). We are God's chosen people.

Another unusual thing about this story is the fact that God already saw them as clean. He rebukes Peter for calling them common and unclean. God says "What I have cleaned, you do not call common." The same applies to you. God has sanctified you and made you very special. You are clean through the blood of Jesus. You are certainly not common, but are unique and greater than you realize. You are His son. You do not have disadvantages but advantages. You have angels around you, and they are sent to serve you *(Heb1:14)*. You are the brother of the Lord Jesus Christ.

YOU ARE ROYALTY

Hebrews 2:9-17, But we see Jesus, who was made a little lower than the angels for the suffering of death, crowned with glory and honor; that He by the grace of God should taste death for every man. For it became Him, for whom are all things, in bringing many sons unto glory, to make the captain of their salvation perfect through sufferings. For both He that sanctifieth and they who are sanctified are all of one: for which cause He is not ashamed to be called their brethren, Saying, I will declare thy name unto my brethren, in the midst of the church will I sing praise unto thee. And again, I will put my trust in Him. And again, Behold I and the children which God has given me. Forasmuch then as the children are partakers of flesh and blood, He also Himself likewise took part of the same; that through death He might destroy him that had the power of death, that is, the devil; And delivered them who through fear of death were all their lifetime subject to bondage. For verily He took not on Him the nature of angels; but He took on Him the seed of Abraham. Wherefore in all things it behooved Him to be made like unto His brethren, that He might be a merciful and faithful High Priest in things pertaining to God, to make reconciliation for the sins of the people.

Hebrew 3:1 goes on to say, Wherefore; holy brethren, partakers of the heavenly calling, consider the Apostle and High Priest of our profession, Christ Jesus.

Do you see what the first verse of Hebrews Chapter three calls you? It states that you are Holy Brethren and Partakers of the Heavenly Calling. You are not common or unclean. You are Holy and have a heavenly calling. You are like Jesus. God the Father has made the two one. Because you are now married to Jesus, are joined to the Lord in one spirit. It is no longer I that live, but Christ Jesus that lives in me. And the life that I now live, I live by the faith of the Son of God who saved me *(Galatians 2:20-21)*. Praise Him forever and ever.

Religion teaches that our purity and our blessings depend on our performance. According to this view, our work would determine our holiness. If we rightly understand what Jesus did on Calvary, though, we know that what He did was enough. When He said it was finished, it was truly finished. The thick veil in the tabernacle that had separated a Holy God from sinful man was torn in two from top to bottom, from heaven to earth, because man could not do this work. God had to tear the veil. This tearing of the veil emphasized that access had been given to every man to boldly approach God. It also made clear that you cannot contain God to a single room. Oh, I get very excited about this! I hope you do as well. Remember, you are not common or unclean. You are holy and sanctified forever. Get rid of that sin conscience once and for all. Your sins, past, present, and future, were dealt with on the cross and the debt Jesus paid was more than enough to wipe your slate clean forever. There is nothing that you can do in Adam that is greater than what God did in Christ (the last Adam) on Calvary.

Hebrews 10:2, tells us that the worshippers (you and I) once purged should have had no more conscience of sins.

We have been purged, but not with the blood of some animal. We were purged with the most precious substance that has ever touched this planet. We have been cleaned by the precious blood of Jesus. Oh, what a Savior!

Do you see that it is important for you to not belittle yourself? A child of God should never be critical of himself or other brothers or sisters. What Jesus did was beyond awesome – it was supernatural! When we speak against one another or put ourselves down, we are trampling on what Jesus did. Do not call what God has cleaned common. You are a royal priesthood. You are a peculiar people. You are kings and priests. You have a heavenly calling because you are children of the Most High. Philemon 6 states that the communication of our faith be effective by the acknowledging of every good thing that is in you. The more you reaffirm who you really are, the more your behavior will change to reflect your true identity. Jesus is in you! You are His temple!

This same Jesus has come for one purpose: that He might be so manifested in us that the world shall see Him, and we must be burning and shining lights to reflect such a holy Jesus.
– Smith Wigglesworth

The Holy Ghost wants you for the purpose of manifesting Jesus through you. Oh may you never be the same again!
– Smith Wigglesworth

Everybody wants to jump in and preach, but bless God, when we are willing to go through with Jesus in that "getting ready" process, then it will be with effectiveness, it will be with power, it will be with the love of God.
– John G. Lake

Chapter Four
JESUS COMES TO HIS TEMPLE

In Mark's gospel, chapter eleven, Jesus comes to the temple three times. This can be a very good illustration of what happens when He comes to make His abode with us. We are the temple now. We are His house that He indwells. Let's look more closely at Mark 11 to learn what we can expect from His coming and the benefits that are ours because we allow Him to have His way in our lives.

First Visit: In Mark 11:5-11, we read that Jesus rode into town on a borrowed donkey. This, in itself, is a fulfillment of prophecy. He came in lowly and submissive to His Father's will. His arrival was marked by people praising Him, saying, "Blessed is He that comes in the name of the Lord. Blessed be the kingdom of our father David that comes in the name of the Lord." They were having an old Pentecostal church meeting – cutting down branches, raising their voices and hands glorifying their Messiah. Jesus then entered the Temple: and when He had looked round about upon ALL THINGS and then he simply leaves. Verse eleven does not say that He taught or did anything. He came in and just looked around at all things. Surely after such an awesome praise service there would be some glorious preaching, but that wasn't done. He just looked around. No one was slain in the Spirit. No one was healed. He just looked around, as if he was inspecting the place. I wonder if He ever just looks around in our services today.

THE REAL MAN IN THE MIRROR

I would like to compare this to when we get born again. Because of what Jesus did for us, we begin to praise Him. Blessed is He that comes in the name of the Lord. In this moment, we think life cannot get any better. The light has illuminated our life; we see the great love that the Father has for us when He sent Jesus to die for us. "While we were yet sinners, Christ died for us" *(Ro 5:8)*. Jesus has come in, and we are praising a sweet meek and lowly Jesus. Blessed is He that comes in the name of the Lord! He is Savior!

Second Visit: Mark 11:12-18, On the following day as he was traveling to the Temple, Jesus was hungry for some fruit. He saw afar off that there was a fig tree having leaves or showing itself as being fruitful. Many churches and Christians do the same today. We want everyone to think we are fruitful even when we are not. Jesus cursed this fig tree because it had no fruit. The only thing that Jesus ever cursed was unproductivity. The original mandate for man found in Genesis is to be fruitful, multiply, replenishes, subdue, and have dominion. This did not change because Adam fell. This is and has always been God's plan for man. It will continue to be His plan throughout our lives here on Earth. God has not changed His mind. We are still to have dominion. When Adam sinned, he covered himself with fig leaves.

After cursing the fig tree, it tells us in verse 15 that they came to Jerusalem, and that Jesus went into the Temple. He then began to cast them out that sold and bought in the temple, and overthrew the tables of moneychangers, and the seats of them that sold doves; And would not suffer that any man should carry any vessel through the temple. This illustrates that man's work is to cease when Jesus comes in. Your salvation is not of works, lest any man should boast. By the sweat of the brow is part of the curse, but Jesus has reversed the curse. You can rest in the finished work of Christ. What has happened to sweet, humble Jesus on this second visit? It looks as if He is having a bad day. He is certainly not the same man that on the previous day everyone was praising. And He taught, saying "Is it not written, MY HOUSE shall be called of all nations the house of prayer? But you have made it a den of thieves." Notice Jesus said "My House." It was also Jesus that said He was building His church and the gates of hell would not prevail. This is the victorious church! Are you part of it?

NO LONGER ON A DONKEY BUT A STALLION!

Jesus did not come this time with a meek spirit. No longer was he riding on a donkey, but a stallion. This time He came with divine authority and took ownership by saying, "this is my house and it is a place of prayer." This means that this is a place where you can have an intimate relationship with God. Then Jesus began tearing up the place and he was overthrowing tables, he was rearranging the furniture. He was casting some things out of the Temple, or His House. Remember, you are His Temple (His House) now. I am not worried about someone building a temple in the Middle East. I could care less about what man is building anywhere in the world. Please do not let a terrorist preacher (one who instills fear in the listener) scare you regarding a temple in Jerusalem. However, I am concerned about letting Jesus have His way in my house, which is actually His Temple. You need to be concerned with your house, too. We have been bought with a precious price, and we are not our own. When Jesus came in first time, He just inspected and looked around at all things, but this time, He came in kicking over things, driving out things, and teaching about a relationship with the Father. There was definitely not much praise going on then. No one was shouting out praises or laying anything down before Him. No glory was being given to Him on this trip. In fact, just the opposite is true. Now the religious system started seeking out ways that they might destroy Him *(Mk11:18)*. There are modern day Pharisees, Scribes, and Sadducees that will seek out ways to destroy the Christ in you, too. Jesus will go against your own religious traditions, but when Truth meets traditions, tradition needs to "bow the knee." Your traditions may keep you from entering the kingdom.

The question we need to ask is whether we will allow Jesus to overthrow our tables and cast out anything that is in us that is not pleasing to Him. In this second visit, Jesus is not only Savior but He is Lord. Jesus is Lord of all. Allow Him to be Lord of your temple. Is Jesus Lord, or is He just a guest that you allow in your house? As a guest, we will give Him a guest room and allow Him to stay, as long as he does not rearrange the furniture. As Lord, we say to Jesus, "Have your WAY, let your WILL BE DONE." Jesus is Lord!

Third Visit: Mark 11:20-28, On the way to the Temple on this morning, the disciples see the fig tree which Jesus cursed. Jesus used it to give a faith lesson, but really it is a lesson on our authority. It is a lesson that teaches us who we really are and what we can really do. Jesus said in Mark 11:22, "have faith in God" (or the God kind of faith). The God kind of faith will speak into nothing and create something. He calls those things which are not, as though they were. Verse 23, For verily I say unto you, that whosoever (not just Jesus, but whosoever, meaning you and I) shall say unto this mountain, be thou removed, and be cast into the sea; and shall not doubt in his heart, but shall believe that those things which HE (you) says shall come to pass; HE (you) shall have whatsoever HE (you) says. Therefore I say unto YOU, what things so ever YOU desire, when YOU pray, believe that YOU receive them, and YOU shall have them. What Jesus was teaching them was that they, too, had authority. If they would simply believe, speak, and pray, they could do the same thing that He did. WOW!

Luke 10: 19, Behold, I give unto you power to tread upon serpents and scorpions, and over all the power of the enemy: and nothing shall by any means hurt you.

On this third visit, in verse 27, And they came again unto Jerusalem: and as He was walking in the Temple, there came to Him the chief priests, and the scribes, and the elders, And say unto Him, By what authority do you do these things? And who gave this authority to you to do these things?

This is so powerful. On the first visit, He inspects the Temple. During His second visit, He cleans house by driving out, flipping over furniture and getting the Temple where prayer (communion) could take place with the Father. He teaches on faith and authority by using the example of the cursed fig tree. But on this third visit, He is now walking in His Temple and the religious rulers want to know by what authority He has to do these things and who gave Him the authority. Here Jesus is KING!

Let me sum this up: If we can allow Him to inspect, rearrange us, cast out the wrong stuff that is in us, He will then walk in His Temple. It will not be you or I operating then but it will be Christ in us that will be walking in His Temple. This is what Paul meant when He said the life that I now live, I live by faith of the Son of God. It was not he that lived but Christ Jesus that was living in Him *(see Ga2:20-21)*. This is being filled with the fullness of God. This is fulfilling our destiny to be like Christ. This is our bodies being used by Jesus Christ to perform His great plans on planet Earth. This is finally the death of Adam, the old man, and living the resurrected life of Christ, the new man. To walk like Jesus, talk like Jesus, be like Jesus which is in reality Jesus walking and operating in His Temple. Jesus is Savior, Jesus is Lord, and Jesus is King!

This exemplifies Jesus being in total control of our bodies which are His Temples. Our bodies are nothing more than a conduit for His power and love to come through. You are a holy vessel designed to carry the Anointed One. When Jesus is walking in His Temple, it is the end of our will being done, but it is His will being done. As it is in heaven, so let it be in earth. If we allow Jesus to change and use us, then we will be used to bring the Father much glory. He will do miracles through you. Signs and wonders shall follow you. Jesus will be walking in His temple, performing the Father's perfect plan for your life which will bring glory to God, the Father. You will impact the world. People will come up to you and question your authority to do these miracles and the person responsible for giving you this authority. You will be able to answer emphatically that I do what I do in the name of Jesus. I preach in His name. I teach in His name. I cast out devils in His name. I heal the sick in

His name. It is all because of the blood of Jesus. I accepted this free gift, given to all men, who call upon Him. Jesus is the Lord of my life. He has given me this power and authority. He has cleansed me and filled me with the precious Holy Spirit, and He has given me power. I am no longer the same. I am now His workmanship. I am a child of God. God indwells me. Greater is He that is in me than he that is in the world. I am a royal priesthood. I am a king that rules and reigns in life by the Lord Jesus Christ.

Before I leave this story completely, let's look at the way the Gospel of Matthew records this same story.

Matthew 21; 12-14, And Jesus went into the temple of God, and cast out all them that sold and bought in the temple, and overthrew the tables of moneychangers, and the seats of them that sold doves, And said unto them, It is written, my house shall be called the house of prayer; but you have made it a den of thieves. And the blind and the lame came to Him in the temple; and He healed them.

I have preached previously from Matthew's account of these three verses and concluded with Purity plus Prayer = Power. Jesus cleansed the Temple (purity). Jesus said His House is a place for communion (prayer), and then the blind and the lame came to be healed (power). Get ready to see the miraculous. Get ready to be used by God in ways that you have only dreamed of when you simply allow Jesus to walk in His Temple. Get ready for the Glory of God (Christ in You) to fill you so you will be unable to stand and minister. It will be Jesus.

What a wonderful thing it would be if there could be groups of believers who would develop this hidden man of the heart until it actually dominated the physical that mortality would be swallowed up of life, God's life. We would be spirit-ruled. Then this hidden man of the heart would govern the reasoning faculties. The senses would be under the dominion of the spirit. The New Creation would rule the physical body.
– E.W. Kenyon

There is a conscious dominion Jesus Christ gives to the Christian soul. It was that thing in the soul of Peter when he met the lame man at the Beautiful Gate. Instead of praying for the man's healing, Peter said, "In the name of Jesus Christ of Nazareth rise up & walk." (Acts 3:6) No prayer about it; no intercession. Peter exercised the dominion that was in his soul & the man instantly arose and went with them into the Temple "walking and leaping and praising God." (Vs 8)
– John G. Lake

Chapter Five

LESSON FROM THE WISE MASTER BUILDER

Solomon is known as the wisest man who has ever lived. 1 Kings 4 and 5 records this account of God giving Solomon this wisdom and the glory which came from it. Solomon built a physical temple for God, and God filled it with His glory. I want to look at what Solomon, the wise Master Builder, did and what God did in response. We are now co-laborers with God, with heaven and earth working together. You are not alone. Jesus, the King of Glory, is with you and the Glory of the latter house (you and I) is greater than the former house. The Bible tells us that Solomon, in all of his glory, was not arrayed like you, but we can learn from him. Wisdom is the principle thing *(Proverbs 4:7)*.

The knowledge of the glory of the Lord is covering the earth as water covers the sea *(Habakkuk 2:14)*. Get ready to be filled with glory. Adam was clothed with Glory. Hebrews 2:7 reveals that God has already crowned you with glory. When Solomon built his temple the glory of God filled the temple so that even the priests could not stand to minister because of this glory cloud. I want people to see Jesus. When we are filled with glory, WE will not be able to minister, but it will be Jesus IN US. It will be the King of glory ministering in our bodies. You will not be standing but it will be the God in you standing up on the inside. This is living in complete communion with the Father as Jesus did. We are one in holy union. Let's look at a few things we can learn from Solomon.

2Chronicles 2:1, And Solomon determined to build a house for the name of the Lord, and a house for His kingdom.

2Chroncles3:1, Then Solomon began to build the house of the Lord...

2Chronicles5:1, Thus all the work that Solomon made for the house of the Lord was finished.

We first see that Solomon had a determination to build a house for the name of the Lord and for his kingdom. It was not for Solomon's name that he had so much determination. It was for the name of the Lord. We must do what we do in the name of the Lord and for His kingdom. Seek ye first the kingdom. Determination and desire are two of the most powerful things we can ever possess. Man can accomplish unbelievable tasks with a spirit of determination and a heart of desire. When Jesus started going to Jerusalem to be crucified, His face was like flint because He would not be denied. For the Joy set before Him, He endured the cross *(Hebrews 12:2)*. He was determined to carry out God's plan. We must be determined to fulfill our purpose, too. We must desire to build in the name of the Lord while extending the kingdom of the Lord here on earth. We all need determination to succeed and become everything that God want us to be – more like Jesus!

Determination by itself will not get anything done alone, though. Faith without works is dead. Not only did Solomon determine to do something, he acted upon in. Chapter 3 verse 1 confirms this. "Then Solomon began to build." You can determine to start going back to school, but if you never enroll you will not graduate. You can determine to start giving more, but if you are not faithful with the little, then you will probably not give the large amount when you receive more. It is not enough just to have a vision of a project. You must get started on the journey to complete the project. You cannot walk a thousand miles without taking that first step. People ask me what they must do to go on a mission trip with me. I tell them that they need to get a passport. You must get started. How do you eat an elephant? The answer is – "one bite at the time." If you have a great vision, then it will require starting, even if it means taking baby steps. Any destination can be reached, even when we take baby steps. Another example of this is building a house. Every house or building first has to have foundation. The foundation is not glorious, but it must be laid. The same principle applies to building what is in your heart. The initial step is getting started. Solomon determined to build so he began building. I want to remind you, though, that Solomon did not have to provide one thing for this temple. It was laid up for him by his father, the previous king. Our Father has provided everything. Jesus, our King, has paid the price in FULL!

Next it tells us that Solomon finished *(2 Chronicles5:1)*. I need this reminder as much as anyone else. I start more projects than I can possibly finish, it is not a good thing. I had actually started three other books before even starting this one. I am great at starting things, but not so great completing them. Do not model my actions in this way. I am praying that I will learn from Solomon. Finish what you have started. Finish your degree. Finish your transcript. Finish what God has put on your heart. Write that book, song, or drama production. Do whatever is in your heart. You can do all things through Christ which strengthens you *(Philippians 4:13)*. You can do great exploits for your Lord Jesus!

In Chapter 5 we find out that Solomon dedicated the temple to the Lord. He gathered the people, he prayed, and he praised God. I like what God did in response to Solomon's actions. Remember, God has commanded a blessing when people get together in unity. Later in this book, (chapter eight) we will discuss the power of unity and the blessing that is found in the cluster (group of as whole.)

2Chronicles5:13-14, It came to pass, as the trumpeters and singers were as one, to make one sound to be heard in praising and thanking the Lord; and of music, and praised the Lord, saying, For He is good; for His mercy endureth for ever: That then the house was filled with a cloud, even the house of the Lord; So that the priests could not stand to minister by reason of the cloud: for the glory of the Lord had filled the house of God.

There is so much in this story. I believe it also to be a prophetic picture of you and I being filled with the King's glory. This happened when the trumpeters and singers were one. This is speaking of our voice: one voice. A trumpet in Solomon's day was not crafted from shining silver or gold. It was a ram's horn. A ram's horn signifies the death of a male ram. Jesus, the Lamb of God, was slain to take away the sin of the world. That is the message that we as His body should declare in unity. There has already been a sacrificial death.

Jesus died in your place. They also sung that the Lord is good and His mercy endures forever. Why do we still have people preaching anything else other than the goodness of the Lord? It is the goodness of the Lord that brings men to repentance *(Romans 2:4)*. God is good all the time and His mercy endures forever. The gospel is truly "GOOD NEWS." Let's tell the world what Jesus did. Let's tell them that God loves them and has reconciled the world unto Himself. It really is amazing grace, how SWEET the Sound!

When they were together, THEN *(vs13)* the house was filled with a cloud. The glory cloud filled the house of God. Jesus ascended in a cloud. Jesus is coming back in a cloud. These are not atmospheric clouds, but people (the spirit realm/glory). Jude vs12, 2 Peter 2:7, and Revelations 1:7 refers to clouds as people. Hebrew 12 reminds us that we are covered about with such a great cloud of witnesses, referring to the saints that have gone on before us. My point is that our traditions have robbed us of present glory. Traditions will keep you from entering the Kingdom. Regardless of your Eschatology, (Sweet Loving Christians will fight you over this!) Jesus is coming and He is coming in and with His people. My teaching is not to change your Eschatological view. I have friends that believe so many different things and I can argue or debate each of them. But all of them cannot possibly be right. To me, Eschatology is not a priority because Jesus said, "Occupy till I come *(Luke 19:13)*." Our job is to be working and taking over while we wait for His coming. He is coming! But now we must work. The word "occupy" is both a business word and military word. We get the word occupation from this word. It also refers to taking over. Our songbook theology has been so wrong on many of fronts. It has instilled a mentality of escapism in the people that should be taking over. To go on our mission trips, we fly way above the clouds. If Jesus is coming back in the atmospheric clouds, then those on the planes will have to come down. If you are in Australia, then up is the Americans down and vice versa. We need to quit thinking with a natural mind. Our minds must be renewed. I do not mean to upset anyone, but when tradition meets truth, tradition needs to bow the knee. Jesus is coming!

Let me say emphatically that I believe in the return of Jesus. Jesus is definitely coming back! This is our blessed hope *(Titus 2:13)*. He may just not be coming in the way that we have been taught that He is returning. He is coming with great glory. Before He comes, let Him make an appearance in you and through you. Open up your house for the King of glory to come into and be ye filled with the Spirit *(Ep5:18)*. Receive the infillings of the Holy Spirit. Dedicate your house to the Lord like Solomon did. God will come into your dedicated house, and you will not be able to minister. It will be Jesus in you. *(Again, read Galatians 2:20-21.)*

Solomon prayed and gave thanks. Some people pray for a visitation, some pray for a habitation while others are praying for manifestations. Instead, we ought to be praying for personification. Let's put on Christ. Reckon the old man dead once and for all. Put on Christ and be filled with the fullness of God. You are truly complete in Him *(Colossians 2:10)*. You are in Him, and He is in you! We are His ambassadors. We are His representatives. Let's re-present Jesus to the world.

There is no limit to the development of the human spirit.
– E.W. Kenyon

Your spirit is the life quality of you, the life principle that gives you action. Not just your mind, but the inbreathed Spirit of God, the breath of God breathed into man. That is eternal. Take this outward man and bury him in the ground, and worms will eat him. But they will not eat the real man – the one that lives within. So few have any conception of giving that inner man his proper place, or recognize his divine right to rule and govern the whole being.
– John G Lake

There is not a human life so poor and small as not to hold many a divine possibility
– James Martineau

Chapter Six
JESUS IS WITH US!

Isaiah 43:1-2, ...Fear not; for I have redeemed thee, I have called thee by thy name; thou art mine. When thou passest through the waters, I will be with thee; and through the rivers, they shall not overflow thee: when thou walkest through the fire, thou shalt not be burned; neither shall the flame kindle upon thee.

I love this passage of scripture. After reading this, anyone can come away with a sense of security. It is a "feel good" passage. God is giving precious promises to us, His children. We get comfort from it because it promises protection. But let's examine this verse more closely. First of all, look at the way he begins. There would be no need for the promise of protection if fear was not present in His children. He opens with "FEAR NOT."

Fear is the opposite of faith. Paul told Timothy that God did not give us a spirit of fear, but one of love, power, and a sound mind. The disciples feared when they were on a ship in the midst of a storm. Jesus was asleep because he had no fear. We are to be like Jesus. Through the words of the prophet Isaiah, God says "Fear not." We have absolutely nothing to fear. Throughout the Bible, God uses this phrase.

Another thing that I want to focus on in this passage is the word "when." It does not say IF you pass through the waters, or IF you walk through the fire. It is clear that it says WHEN. This means that you will face some tests. You will, at some point go "through the fire." There will be times that you go through "the waters and the river." However, this is not bad news but very good news. The gospel is always good news. Isaiah's prophecy here is telling of a three- fold deliverance.

GREAT DELIVERANCE

When the prophet Isaiah was speaking, he was prophesying to the children of Israel, the Jews. He was speaking by inspiration of the Holy Spirit when he mentioned "passing through the waters." In the listener's mind, they had to think back to when God delivered them out of Egypt and they crossed the Red Sea on dry ground. Volumes of books have been and will continue to be written about this great deliverance out of Egypt because of the great things in this story. I only want to emphasize a few.

First of all, God always uses a man with a message. God used Moses to speak to Pharaoh and to the children of Israel. God has given you a message to deliver to people, also. During the deliverance, Moses is leading the people out of Egypt, when Pharaoh changes his mind and pursues after them. *(Read Exodus chapters 14-15.)* The children of Israel are in a very vulnerable position. Exodus 14:2 states "that the wilderness had shut them in." The Red Sea was before them, the mountains and wilderness on both sides, and Pharaoh's army was behind them. In this dire situation, the people began to cry out to God and talk about their pastor Moses. They began to murmur and complain, blaming Moses saying "because there had been no graves in Egypt. Have thou taken us away to die in this wilderness." They would have certainly returned to slavery if God had not sent them a true deliverer. Please saints of God, learn how to hold your tongue when speaking of a man of God.

Moses tells the people to "Fear not, stand still, and see the salvation of the Lord." Oh, how we need to do the same today! Fear not, have faith, stand still, enter into rest from your labors, and behold the Lamb of God. He goes on to explain in verse 13, referring to the Egyptians (their masters, enemies), "You shall see them no more." When you finally CROSS over, you will not see your enemies. Your enemy has already been defeated. Your enemy has been disarmed. Your enemy has been spoiled by Jesus. This means getting out of bondage forever. Say goodbye to your taskmaster. You will surely see them no more.

In Verse 15, the Lord said unto Moses, Wherefore (WHY) are you crying out to Me? Speak unto the children of Israel, that they go forward: But lift up your rod and stretch out your hand over the sea and divide it: and the children of Israel shall go on dry ground through the midst of the sea.

In this passage God asks Moses," Why are you crying out to me?" I believe that there are times when He asks us the same question. When a child cries, most parents will pick the baby up to comfort them to get them to stop crying. But when a child reaches a certain age and then begins to cry, parents will simply tell them to stop crying. You are not a baby anymore. So suck up those tears. You have grown up, both physically and now spiritually. We need maturity in the body of Christ. It is imperative to stop crying and complaining about everything that is wrong and start taking authority over it.

Galatians 4:1-2, Now, I say, That the heir, as long as he is a child, differs nothing from a servant, though he be lord of all; but is under tutors and governors until the time appointed of the father.

You are heirs of God and joint heirs with Jesus Christ *(Romans 8:17)*.

We will never get our inheritance as long as we are children. When my boys were younger, they could not drive my cars until they became a certain age and had developed a level of maturity. Because they are my heirs they will have everything that is mine one day. However, there are certain things that they could not possess until they have shown competence. One example is shooting my guns. You would not want to give something with that much power to a child because they could get hurt. Today my boys can go hunting by themselves. They have grown up, but when they were younger, they needed supervision of an adult. You are not going to let an adolescent drive alone until they have matured and demonstrated that they are good drivers. As children we all need the SUPERVISION that God has for us. Remember, He sees the end from the beginning. We do not stay children forever. God is calling us to maturity so that we can receive and operate with our authority, enjoying our inheritance. We need to have "grow up" mentality instead of a "go up" mentality. Grow-up before you go up!

God told Moses to quit crying and lift up HIS ROD, USING HIS

AUTHORITY! God told Moses for him to part the water, too. Can you imagine the pressure this put on Moses? The people's deliverance depended on Moses – his faith and his God given authority. Are there people today depending upon your faith and authority? God told Moses to tell the people to go forward. It is no time to back up, but we simply must go forward. Do not look back because that is not the direction in which you are headed. You are to go forward, learn to use your authority, speak to your own mountain (obstacle), and command it to move out of your way.

Philippians 3:13-14, …forgetting those things which are behind, and reaching forth unto those things which are before, I press toward the mark for the prize of the high calling of God in Christ Jesus.

Well, you know what happened. Moses lifted up his rod, the waters parted, and the people went over on dry ground. The army behind them drowned in the RED (Blood) SEA. You have crossed over and now you have an inheritance that you need to receive by faith in Jesus. Jesus has already spoiled principalities and defeated our enemies. They cannot cross the blood. When Isaiah, the prophet, spoke of passing through the waters, it was this picture of the great deliverance that they remembered.

RECEIVE YOUR INHERITANCE!

Isaiah 43:2, When thou passest through the waters, I will be with thee; and through the rivers, they shall not over flow thee: when thou walk through the fire, thou shalt not be burned; neither shall the flame kindle upon thee.

Isaiah, the prophet, also spoke of the rivers not overflowing them. Again, he was speaking to Israelites so in their mind, they had to think of Joshua as Savior leading their people across the river Jordon at flood stage to inherit their promise land. This is the second deliverance that Isaiah is speaking of. This is found in Joshua Chapter three and four. Please read because as with Moses leading the children of Israel across the Red Sea there is so much in this story also that I cannot write about it all. I just want to bring out a few things. My Pastor, Dr. Paul Harthern, has an excellent teaching on Joshua that I would recommend to anyone. Because of time and space, I only want to bring out a few things.

Jordon means descender or death. Your low places will reveal God's great love for you. God is with you in the low places. The low places produce more miracles. Yea, though I walk through the valley of the shadow of death, I will fear no evil: for Thou art with me; thy rod and thy staff they comfort me *(Ps 23:4)*. Death has lost its sting and grave the victory *(1Corinthians 15:55)*. You died at Calvary. You were crucified with Christ. Your Savior, Jesus Christ, has led us to our inheritance. After they crossed the Jordon, Joshua had twelve men, a leader from each tribe, to bring up stones from the river for a memorial. They were to tell their children and their grandchildren what this meant. That is why I am sure that when Isaiah was prophesying, the listener was reflecting on this. When the priests bearing the ark touched the waters, the waters of the Jordon rolled back to a city named Adam and the children crossed over on dry ground. What a miracle, what a Savior! Before them was their inheritance and behind them were the dead masters of Egypt. It is funny to me that after they had crossed over, the river returned to its original place. It was as if God told them saying, "You are not going back. I will not let you." Praise His name!

Ephesians 1:3,11, Blessed be the God and Father or our Lord Jesus Christ, who hath (past tensed) blessed us with all spiritual blessings in heavenly places in Christ: 11, In Whom also we have obtained (again past tensed) an inheritance, being predestinated according to the purpose of Him who worketh all things after the counsel of His own will.

We are now in Christ. We have obtained an inheritance. We are seated with Him in heavenly places *(Ep. 2:6)*. If any man be in Christ, he is a new creature: old things are passed away; behold, all things are become new *(2 Co.5:17)*.

After Joshua and the children of Israel went over on dry ground into the land of their inheritance, Joshua was told to circumcise all the males. This signified entering into covenant. Covenant is very powerful and I will discuss this briefly later. God is a covenant God. The Israelites did this at a place called Gilgal, which means my reproach has been rolled away. Can you see the amazing grace of God toward you? Our Savior, Jesus Christ, has rolled away your reproach. Everything that God had against you, He took out on Calvary's cross. Your reproach has been rolled away. You can now enjoy your inheritance. The children of Israel had to lose their slave mentality. It took another generation to inherit the land. Only Joshua and Caleb from the previous generation were able to enjoy the land. They had a different spirit because they had faith. They believed God. We must too lose that slave or servant mentality, and put on a "son" mentality. Jesus said in John 15:15, "I know longer call you servants." We are in His family now. We are sons, and the whole earth is waiting for us, even groaning for our appearing. Can you believe like Caleb and Joshua, or will you die off in the wilderness of religion, never inheriting all that belongs to you on this side?

On a side note: Why don't we believe anymore? When we were children, we believed. Jesus said, "if you want to enter the kingdom you must be like a little child." Why is it that when we become adults that we are so skeptical? God called us to be BELIEVERS, but we question everything. We try to discern and analyze everything instead of simply believing. All things are possible to them that believe. Have faith in God! Do not fear, but simply believe. Some people have more faith in the devil's ability to deceive than God's power to keep you. If you BELIEVE, You will RECEIVE and ACHIEVE. If you DOUBT, you will POUT and go WITHOUT.

Get ready to walk in the fullness of your inheritance. Get ready to cross over from lack to abundance. Get ready to go from sickness to walking in divine health. Get ready to fulfill your destiny and walk like Jesus, talk like Jesus, and be like Jesus. Get ready to do the works that Jesus did and even greater. Are you ready? It is your destiny.

I AM NOT SMELLING LIKE SMOKE

There is an additional deliverance that Isaiah speaks about in this passage.

Isaiah 43:2…, when thou walketh through the fire, thou shalt not be burned; neither shall the flame kindle upon thee.

Again, the audience here was Jews so they probably remembered the story that was told concerning three Hebrew boys that would not bow to a false god. Shadrach, Meshach, and Abednego were three men that had conviction and would not bow to an idol "made with hands." The king Nebuchadnezzar got very angry and threw them into a fiery furnace. He was furious and commanded that they should heat up the furnace seven times more than it would have been normally (Daniel 3:19). Seven is a number of completion or fullness. This should have been a complete destruction. The three men were bound and then thrown into the fire. The furnace was so hot that the men who threw them in died immediately, just from the heat of the flames.

Verse 24 says, Then Nebuchadnezzar the king was astonished, and rose up in haste, and spake, and said unto his counselors, Did not we cast three men bound into the midst of fire? They answered and said unto the king, True, O king. He answered and said, Lo, I see four men loose, walking in the midst of the fire, and they have no hurt; and the form of the fourth is like the Son of God.

I love this story of deliverance. Three men were thrown into the fire. We are a triune being. We were bound completely, and the fire was completely hot. But Jesus went into the fire with us, we came out, not burned, not even smelling like smoke. We came out loose and free because whom the Son sets free is free indeed. No weapon formed against you shall prosper *(Isaiah 54:17)*. Jesus said, I will never leave you nor forsake you. I will walk in the fire with you. I will protect you as you go into the entire world. I am with you until the end. All power is given me in heaven and earth, Go YOU therefore into all the world and make disciples of all nations and lo, I am with you always *(Matthew 28:18-20)*. The Great Commission is found in all four gospels and also in the book of Acts.

God has a purpose for us all and has given this great commission to us all. It is not the great suggestion, but it is our job to do while we are on earth. I hope you are involved in a ministry that is reaching the world. If not, I give you a personal invitation to join with me and our covenant partners who are making an impact through GRAB Ministries (Gospel Reaching All Borders.) The world does not need to see just another preacher or just another religion. They need to see Jesus, and they can see Him through you. He is the fourth man that is with you. No matter what we may go through, it cannot compare with what we have been through already with Jesus at Calvary. Paul had a great revelation of the work of Jesus on the cross and how it changed us for His glory.

The instant you believe you become a possessor of the Father's nature. You become as much as a child of God as Jesus was in His earth walk. You may not have developed; you may not have grown in grace and in the knowledge of the Word; you may not have taken advantage of your privileges as a son; but you are a son, an heir of God and a joint heir with Christ. Until we recognize that we are New Creations, the very sons and daughters of God, we will never take our place.

– E.W. Kenyon

This is no mere self-centered, self-complacent experiences of blessings. It is something that leads to practical results and accomplishes definite things. There is power in it. It takes hold of God until something is done. If God is reigning in us, He will rule over everything around us. If we have the Holy Spirit within us, we will see the providence of God in His marvels of answered prayer and accomplish results.

– A.B. Simpson

Chapter Seven
PAUL'S REVELATION

Other than Jesus Christ Himself, no one has impacted Christianity more than the great Apostle Paul. This great apostle wrote over half of the New Testament. Paul, who was born Saul of Tarsus, was a religious devil (man) before his conversion to Christianity. He persecuted the church and had men and women of faith killed. Finally, Jesus revealed Himself to Saul and he was converted. This changed him completely. Our conversion should also produce a change. You can read about his conversion in Acts 9. After he was converted he went to Arabia and later to Damascus. He explains his experience in Galatians 1:12, For I neither received it (his gospel) of man, neither was I taught it, but by revelation of Jesus Christ. Let us look further on how Paul received his great revelation.

Galatians 1:15-2:2a, But when it pleased God, who separated me from my mother's womb, and called me by His grace, To reveal His Son in me, that I might preach Him among the heathen; immediately I conferred not with flesh and blood: Neither went I up to Jerusalem to them that which were apostles before me; but I went into Arabia, and returned again unto Damascus. Then after three years I went up to Jerusalem to see Peter, and abode with him fifteen days. But other apostles saw I none, save James the Lord's brother. Now the things which I write unto you, behold before God, I lie not. Afterwards I came to Syria and Cilicia; And was unknown by face unto the churches of Judea which were in Christ: But they heard only, That he which persecuted us in times past now preaches the faith which once he destroyed. And they glorified God in me. Then fourteen years after I went up again to Jerusalem with Barnabas and took Titus with me also. And I went up by revelation, and communicated unto them that gospel which I preach among the Gentiles, but privately to them which were of reputation, lest by any means I should run, or had run, in vain.

This is truly amazing to me. Why would this new believer not want to go immediately in fellowship with the other Apostles? Was it because they would not believe him and knew that he had formerly persecuted the church? Was Paul afraid of them and vice versa? I do not think that was the reasons. I am going to share my own opinion here about why I feel that he did not discuss this with any man. You might disagree with this, but I believe his conversion was so radical that he had to be alone to sort it all out. He probably even questioned his sanity. Can you picture that? After years of studying religion under the best teacher of that day, he flipped sides instantly. After being on top of his class and more zealous than any other, he finds out that what he has believed was a total lie. This Jesus proved Himself to Paul that He was indeed Lord. The same people that he had murdered were right in their convictions and he was wrong. Just knowing that he killed innocent men and women was enough for him to feel so many different emotions. Paul's world had turned upside down. Or you could say right side up! Can you imagine the change that took place? He had to sort it all out. Regardless or the reason, he did not communicate his feelings with any man for at least three years.

1 John 4:20; 27, But you have an unction from the Holy One and you know all things (you ole know it all). But the anointing which you have received of Him abides in you, and you need not that any man teach you: but the same anointing teaches you of all things, and is truth, and is no lie, and even as it hath been taught you, you shall abide in Him.

I am a man that has been educated by men so I believe in using the avenue of education to improve our knowledge. God has put teachers in the body of Christ to teach us. It is a good thing to get teaching from someone who knows more than you. A disciple is a learner and we are Disciples of Christ. We should strive to constantly be learning. But some things are better caught than taught. In the beginning, Adam did not have a University of Eden. There was no Eden High School. There was not even a Primary or Elementary School. Adam walked with God and discerned from His Spirit. If Adam needed to know anything, he got his answer from God. One day, God wanted to see what Adam would name the animals, and Adam named them all. Have you ever wondered where Adam got the names? Adam and God's Spirit were in perfect communion with one another. The Holy Spirit is the best teacher that has ever existed, and it was He that taught Adam. A great teacher will get even the most intellectually challenged student to learn. What Paul received was not taught in seminary or in a natural classroom. Paul's revelation came to him by the Spirit of God. I love fresh revelation. John is writing that the Holy Spirit is with you, abiding in you. You have the Teacher living in you. What Paul got was fresh revelation from the throne room of God, taught to Him by the Spirit of the Lord. Jesus came to restore man's relationship with God. The Spirit now is again speaking to our spirits that we are the children of God. This is certainly not all of Paul's revelation, but I want to share a 6-fold revelation that I have received from Paul's teaching here.

1. WE WERE CRUCIFIED WITH CHRIST:
Galatians 2:20, I am crucified with Christ: nevertheless I live; yet not I, but Christ lives in me: and the life that I now live in the flesh I live by the faith of the Son of God, who love me, and gave Himself for me. I do not frustrate the grace of God: for if righteousness came by the law, then Christ is dead in vain.

Revelation number one is that you were crucified with Christ. You do not have to kill yourself. You are already dead. Reckon the old man dead. Bury Him so that you can go on living the abundant life. Colossians 3:3 reminds us "for you are dead, and your life is hid with Christ in God." *(See also Colossians 2:20)* You cannot rehabilitate the old man. You cannot educate him or dress him up to look good. He is dead! Reckon him dead once and for all and have a funeral service in his honor.

2. WE WERE BURIED WITH CHRIST:
Colossians 2:12 state we are buried with Him in baptism. Baptism is a symbol of going down as one man, but coming up as a new man. I love baptismal services. The old man is being buried, and the new man is coming forth out of the tomb.

Ephesians 2:4-5, But God who is rich in mercy, for His great love wherewith He loved us, Even when we were dead in sins, hath quickened us together with Christ.

3. WE WERE RESURRECTED WITH CHRIST:

Colossians 2:12, Buried with Him in baptism, wherein also you are raised with Him through the faith of the operation of God, who hath raised Him from the dead.

Romans 8:11 But if the same Spirit that raised up Jesus from the dead dwell in you, He that raised up Christ from the dead shall also quicken your mortal bodies by His Spirit that dwells in you.

Ephesians 2:1, And You hath He quickened (made alive), who were dead in trespasses and sins.

Ephesians 2:6, And hath raised us up together...

Colossians 3:1, If you then be risen with Christ, seek those things which are above, where Christ sits on the right hand of God.

We can live the resurrected life if we can only receive this revelation that the old man is dead, and we have been raised with Christ as a brand new man.

4. WE ASCENDED WITH CHRIST:

Ephesians 4:7-13, But unto every one of us is given grace according to the measure of the gift of Christ. Wherefore He saith, When He ascended up on high, He led captivity captive, and gave gifts unto men. (Now that He ascended, what is it but that He also descended first into the lower parts of the earth? He that descended is the same that ascended up far above all heavens, that He might fill all things.) And He gave some, apostles; and some, prophets;

and some, evangelists; and some, pastors and teachers; For the perfecting of the saints, for the work of the ministry, for the edifying of the body of Christ: Till we all come in the unity of the faith, and of the knowledge of the Son of God, unto a perfect man, unto the measure of the stature and fullness of Christ. (See also Ephesians 1:17-2:6)

5. WE ARE SEATED WITH CHRIST:

Ephesians 2:6, And hath raised us up together, and made us sit together in heavenly places in Christ.

Revelation 3:21, To him that overcomes will I grant to sit with Me in my throne, even as I also overcame, and am set down with my Father in His throne.

This is so amazing! It confirms that we have been blessed with all spiritual blessings in heavenly places in Christ *(Ephesians 1:3)*.

6. WE ARE TO RULE AND REIGN WITH CHRIST:

Romans 5:17, For if by one man's offence death reigned by one; much more they which receive abundance of grace and of the gift of righteousness shall reign in life by one, Jesus Christ. (See also Revelation 3:21)

This really has to do with simply being in Christ. I would suggest that you do a study of how often you will find this phrase "in Christ" in Paul's writings. You will be surprised. You are in Christ, and He is in you. Your peace is found in Him, your joy is found in Him, your power is found in Him. Apart from Him, we can do nothing but with Him, we can do all things through Christ which strengthens us. This is definitely not all of Paul's revelation, but if we can get just this part of it, it will change our perspective on life, giving us security to face any giant that stands in our way. Jesus is with us. I am in Him. He is in me. Together we are one. He that is joined to the Lord is one spirit *(1Corinthians 6:17)*. You are married to Him. There is no longer two, but one. When I finished making my coffee this morning, I added both sugar and cream. After I stirred these ingredients, the coffee became a new creation. I could not separate the coffee from the sugar, nor could I take out the sugar from the coffee. It had become a new creation. So it is with us. Christ has added His sweetness to our black, bitter soul and we cannot separate the two. He has made us white as snow. He has filled us with Himself and His great love. Stir up the gift of God in you. Amazing grace, how sweet the sound that saved a wretch like me. I once was lost, but NOW I am found! Thank you, Lord Jesus. *(See Isaiah 1:18-19)* It is a personal invitation from God.

Before closing this teaching, meditate on Ephesians 1:17-23, a prayer that Paul prayed when he was praying for the church at Ephesus. This was a Holy Spirit inspired prayer. If it was good enough for the early Christians at Ephesus, then it is certainly needed for us today. Let me highlight some points in this prayer.

1. He prayed that we may know God. *(V 1:17)*
2. He prayed that a spirit of wisdom be given to us *(v 17)*
3. He prayed that our eyes of our understanding be opened *(v 18)*
4. He prayed that we may know what is the hope of His calling *(v 8)*

5. He prayed that we may know the riches of the glory of his inheritance in the saints. *(v18)*
6. He prayed that we would know the exceeding great power given to us who believe. *(v19)*
7. He wants us to know what Jesus did for us to receive this power, and the victory HE won. *(v 19-23)*

I challenge you to read this prayer daily along with the one in Chapter 3:14-21. This prayer is inspired by the Holy Spirit and it was canonized into our holy scriptures. Try substituting your name in place of "You" or "your" so you can make these prayers personal. I cannot emphasize enough the value that these two prayers have had on my life. Just as with many other prayers in the Bible, if you make them personal, you will see a great change begin to take place in you. You are not a victim, but a victor. You are not underprivileged, but privileged. You have angels surrounding you. You have God in you with the promise from Him that He would never leave you. You are forgiven and redeemed. You have been bought with the precious blood of Jesus.

Romans 8:32 says, He that spared not His own Son, but delivered Him up for us all, how shall He not WITH HIM also freely give us all things?

You are the salt of the earth and the light of the world. You are the ambassador from heaven. You are the representative of Jesus here on earth. You are to RE-PRESENT Jesus to the world. Can you see Him? If not, please keep praying these prayers. The Light will shine in the darkness. This is your destiny. This is your high calling.

Your life has a divine purpose. To fulfill your purpose, Jesus must be all in all inside of you. He must be Savior, Lord, and King! God has great plans for your life. If all of this seems too good to be true, or if you are still in doubt, realize that you really had nothing to do with it. It is all by the amazing grace of God. It is unmerited favor. It's all because of Jesus and His shed blood. It is all because of the Father's great love that He has for us. To get a full presentation of Christ, then we must be joined with other believers. Together we are the Body of Christ. We need each other. We are not islands, so we are told to not forsake the assembling of ourselves together. There is a commandment from God to bless unity *(Psalms 133)*. If we want the fullness of God's blessing in our lives then we will let nothing separate us from other family members (the church).

For the thirst is of God, the desire is of God, the plan is of God, the purpose is of God. God's plan, God's thought, God's vessel, and God's servant. We are in the world to meet every need, but not of the world or its spirit. God incarnate in humanity. We become partakers of the divine nature to manifest the life of Jesus to the world.
– Smith Wigglesworth

Satan separates; God unites; love binds us together.
– D.L. Moody

We must indeed all hang together, or, most assuredly, we shall all hang separately.
– Benjamin Franklin

He who abides in me, and I in him, bears much fruit: for without Me you can do nothing.
– Jesus, John 15:5

Chapter Eight
THE NEW WINE IS IN THE CLUSTER!

When I was young in the Lord and had just accepted the call of God upon my life, my dreams and visions were focused on the world. I was so on fire. I was young, ambitious, and zealous, but had very little wisdom. This fire was fueled even more when I would read books of the early fathers of our faith that described their great exploits for God. Heroes of mine like Smith Wigglesworth, John G. Lake, John and Howard Carter, Oral Roberts, William Seymour, John and Charles Wesley, John Knox, D.L. Moody, E.W. Kenyon, Kenneth Hagan, and many more were my role models. These men shook the world and brought heaven to earth. I wanted to be like them, but I did not think that I needed anyone but my Lord Jesus. Jesus and I together were going to conquer the world. During the following years, I learned that I cannot do anything really by myself. I need my family, my church, and my covenant partners. I need the wisdom of men of God that are around me and over me in the Lord. True covenant relationships are priceless. You cannot put a value on true friends and true covenant partners.

Isaiah 65:8, "Thus saith the Lord, As the new wine is found in the cluster, and one saith, Destroy it not; for a blessing is in it...

I really have grown to love this powerful verse of scripture. The One speaking is the Lord. I know that all scripture is inspired by the Lord, but when, "Thus saith the Lord," is emphasized then maybe we should pay closer attention. The new wine (anointing, blessing) is in the cluster. Together we are much stronger than we are by ourselves. No one in the Body of Christ is to be alone. Even the Lone Ranger had Tonto, Batman had Robin, and Superman had Lois Lane. When God created the heaven and the earth, everything was described as "very good." The first thing that is mentioned in the Bible that was not good was man being alone (Genesis 2:18). The new wine is in the cluster.

The Bible says much about the New Wine. Remember, I mentioned previously about the importance of the offering. The Bible records that God wants us to bring the offering of the new wine, which is in the cluster *(Nehemiah 10:39)*. In Matthew 9:17 and Mark 2:22, we are taught that we cannot put new wine into old bottles or wineskins because it is so powerful that the bottles will break. The bottles and the wine would then be wasted. God wants the offering of the new wine, as it is extremely valuable to God. On Pentecost, some thought the Spirit-filled believers were full of New Wine *(Acts 2:13)*. The new wine was in the cluster, and there was a blessing in it.

No man is to attempt going alone. When Jesus sent the disciples out, He sent them out in pairs. I do not like to acknowledge the devil anywhere or anytime because he has already been defeated on the cross and spoiled. However, the one thing that I can say about Satan is that he works very hard to divide God's people. People are divided by race, color, socioeconomic factors, denominations, education, political parties, and etcetera. The Bible tells us that a house divided cannot stand. It may be that Satan knows the awesome power of a united people. If one can put a thousand to flight, and two ten thousand, then what can an army marching in rank and file do? What can your local congregations do? Being in unity manifests God's power in a way that we don't seem to fully understand.

Psalms 133, Behold, how good and how pleasant it is for brethren to dwell together in unity! It is like the precious ointment upon the head, that ran down upon the beard, even Aaron's beard: that went down to the skirts of his garments; As the dew of Hermon, and as the dew that descended upon the mountains of Zion: for there the Lord commanded the blessing, even life for evermore.

This command by God blesses unity. Whenever we are together in unity Jesus is with us. When we are in a covenant relations, Jesus promises to be there. Peter tells us that our prayers can be hindered just from not being in agreement with our spouse. Maybe that is why the Bible teaches that if you have anything against anyone, then you should go make it right before laying your worship on the altar.

Matthew 18:18-20, Verily I (Jesus) say unto you, Whatsoever YOU shall bind on earth shall be bound in heaven: and whatsoever you shall loose on earth shall be loosed in heaven. Again I say unto you, that if two of you shall agree on earth as touching anything that they shall ask, it shall be done for them of my Father which is in heaven. For where two or three are gathered together in my name, there am I in the midst of them.

Whenever there is an agreement by two or three, then Jesus said that He would be there. No matter where "there" is, Jesus is there and that is where the blessing will be also.

One of the great characteristics of the powerful early church was their unity. You see it throughout the book of Acts. They had many things in common. They were together in one place, and they were one mind with one purpose. This is especially true in the opening chapters. Did you know that Acts is the only book of the Bible that does not have a conclusion? It is as if the writer picked up his pen, and took a break, but with every intention of returning to it. Why? The reason is that it is still being written. The Acts of the Holy Spirit is still going on today. We are some of its latest chapters. The Holy Spirit is still working through you and I.

Let's look at one of the earlier reference of unity in the church.

Acts 2:42-47, And they continued stedfastly in the apostle's doctrine and fellowship, and in breaking of bread, and in prayers. And fear came upon every soul: and many wonders and signs were done by the apostles. And all that believed were together, and had all things common; And sold their possessions and goods, and parted them to all men, as every man had need. And they, continuing daily with one accord in the temple, and breaking bread from house to house, did eat their meat with gladness and singleness of heart, praising God, and having favor with all the people. And the Lord added to the church daily such as should be saved.

The results of this unity from this short passage are many:
1. The Apostles did many great miracles and wonders.

2. The people praised God.
3. God received glory.
4. The people were filled with joy. The joy of the Lord is your strength *(Nehemiah 8:10)*.
5. The Lord added to the church daily.

I enjoy traveling and especially love missionary work. I usually go to Asia several times a year, as well as traveling to Africa and Central America. I will travel wherever I feel the Lord's leading me. What I love about other countries is the unity among different Christian groups that they have. Baptists and Pentecostals are working together, along with the Methodists, Catholics, Anglicans, Presbyterians, AOGs, COGs and many other groups. It seems that all denominations and independent groups are working closely together, unlike most of the churches here in the USA. In some instances, they simply have to work together because Christians are in such a minority.

I remember a conference I did in northern India where Christians are persecuted often and definitely are in the minority. This was a large conference in which we trained leaders during the day, but we had revival meetings at night. There were several groups and denominations represented. The evening crowed was very large. One particular night, the praise and worship service really became boisterous and heartfelt. It was "smoking," if you know what I mean. There was such a tangible presence of God that came into our mist. One particular group was dancing wildly, radically praising and worshiping. They were filled with the new wine. The leader of the group seemed to be unusually boisterous. I turned to my friend on the stage and asked, "Are those charismatics?" He answered that they were Baptist, which really surprised me. In South Georgia, where I live, most Baptist is very conservative in their worship. However, in India this particular group's pastor had been led to the Lord by a Baptist missionary so he called himself a Baptist, too. When the missionary left the country, the pastor read in the Word of God that David danced before the Lord with all his might. He also learned that David was a man after God's own heart. While reading the Bible the importance of praise and worship was revealed to him. Therefore, he was not shy about his love for His King. Because he only had the Word of God and the Spirit of God leading him, he worshipped the way that he thought God wanted. I wonder how different our worship would be if it wasn't for traditions. Most of what we do has been taught and passed down by man. The Father is looking for those that will worship Him in spirit and in truth. I believe this Baptist pastor had perfect praise. I believe that God was pleased with His unified church that night. There were many miracles and healings done in the name of Jesus. We were all together in one place and one mind. Jesus was King! I will always have very fond memories of that night, especially the way God made His presence known.

I am often asked why we see miracles over-seas, but we do not see them here. My answer is that we do see them here, but just not as often. If we get together, truly unified, then I do believe we would see many more. Why do we see miracles at all? It is all because of what Jesus did on the cross. He has restored man to God. Man is again His chief operator on the earth. He has placed His power inside of man. In the next chapter we will discuss how to release this power He has given us.

We need to remember that the new wine is found in the cluster. God wants the offering of the new wine. On Pentecost, they were filled with the Spirit. They were together in one place and one mind. Can we also have a move of God in our meetings? You bet we can. All we have to do is get together in agreement. There is a command blessing found in unity. The anointing is there, and the Anointed One is there. The power to break and destroy any yoke is inside of you, so we are victorious! To see others move from defeat to victory, we must learn to release the heavenly treasure that is in us.

There is a conscious dominion Jesus Christ gives to the Christian soul. It was that thing in the soul of Peter when he met the lame man at the Beautiful Gate. Instead of praying for the man' healing, Peter said, "in the name of Jesus Christ of Nazareth rise up and walk" (Acts3:6). No prayer about it; no intercession. Peter exercised the dominion that was in his soul. The divine flash of the power of God went forth from his soul, and the man instantly arose and went into the Temple "walking and leaping , and praising God" (v.8).
– John G. Lake

A non-miracle gospel is reduced to a purely spiritual religion, ineffective on earth.
– Reinhard Bonnke

Chapter Nine

POWER RELEASING PRINCIPLES

Jesus said in Acts 1:8 that we would receive power after the Holy Spirit would come upon us. Luke 10:19 also reveals that He has given us power to tread on serpents, scorpions and over all the power of the enemy. The Word also tells us in 2 Corinthians 5:20 that we are the ambassadors for Christ. Paul reminds us in *1 Corinthians 4:19 – 20, But I will come to you shortly, if the Lord will, and will know, not the speech of them which are puffed up, but the POWER. For the Kingdom of God is not in word, but in power.*

It is my firm belief that we need a demonstration of the power of God in the earth today. I believe it is an indictment against us that we do not see more miracles and power demonstrated. We need more demonstration than declaration. In other words, we need the demonstration to back up our declaration. Paul acknowledge the same thing when he told the Corinthians in *1 Corinthians. 2:4-5, And my speech and my preaching was not with enticing words of man's wisdom, but in demonstration of the Spirit and of POWER: That your faith should not rest in the wisdom of men, but in the POWER of God.*

If a man can talk you into something then someone else that is more eloquent and persuasive can talk you out of it. Man's wisdom is good, but there is always someone who has a fresher revelation and even more wisdom. If you were never trained by man in spiritual things and you picked up the Bible for yourself to read and study (what an innovative thought), you would still come away with the sense that our God is definitely powerful. You would see that He is a supernatural God. There is no way that you could come away from reading and studying the Bible to even consider that God does not perform miracles. You would also know that the church has power after reading about the miracle the workers in the Body of Christ demonstrate. Therefore, you would realize that you have power, too, and that you should be operating in the power of God. The thought that God doesn't do miracles anymore wouldn't even enter your mind yet many are taught that miracles stopped when He Himself said, "I am the Lord, I change not." If a man believes that God doesn't do miracles now, then that man has been taught by someone who is spiritually blind and he himself is also blind. That is an example of the blind leading the blind. Jesus said if the blind leads the blind, then they will both fall in a ditch *(Matthew 15:14)*. A ditch is nothing more than a grave with both ends knocked out. Religion without relationship with the Omnipotent God will destroy you.

Hebrews declares loudly that Jesus Christ is the same yesterday, today, and forever. If He had a healing anointing yesterday, then He still has it today. If He did miracles yesterday, then He would still be performing them today. Your faith should not rest in the wisdom of men, but instead in the power of the Almighty God. You were also given power! There are two main Greek words to describe the power given to you. We get the word authority from one (Exousia), and power is translated from the other (Dunamis). God has given you both the authority and the power to operate in the supernatural.

The deputy's badge gives him authority, but it's his gun that gives him the power to back up his authority. At any time (because of the power given to him) the deputy can stop traffic, and require a number of things because he has delegated authority. He also has the power or the means to do his job and carry out his duty.

Like the deputy that has been given delegated authority, also you have been given delegated authority. He has been given the power to carry out his own authority just as you have been given special power to carry out your duties. I have seen many miracles, but I want to see so many more. I have always been attracted to the power of God. I want to understand more of His power and especially how to release the power that the Bible tells me that we have. 1 John 4:4 assures us that Greater is He that is in you, than he that is in the world. The primary focus of this book is to encourage you to show the world Jesus, and if we are to do that, then we must manifest Jesus.

Acts 10:38, How God anointed Jesus of Nazareth (the man from the little town not the God from heaven) with the Holy Ghost and with power: who went about doing good, and healing all that were oppressed of the devil; for God was with him.

Is God with you or not? According to 2 Corinthians 4:7, 10-11, we are to be manifesting Jesus in our bodies. 1 Corinthians 12:7 also declares that the manifestations (outward displays) of the Spirit are given to every man to profit. If Jesus is the same today, and He went a about doing good, healing all that were oppressed of the devil, should not we be doing the same today as His representative?

If we are, then just like the deputy, we need additional training on handling this power effectively.

Throughout the years I have questioned God why some people gets healed and why others do not. Some things we may never know, but we should continue to seek after the things of God. Ignorance is certainly no excuse for not trying. I am seeing more miracles today because I believe that we must learn how to operate in the anointing. We progress toward the mark, or our destiny. We can learn how to release the power. There are many keys and principle that help us operate in the kingdom. Jesus said that He has given us the keys to the kingdom. Therefore, we have everything we already need to operate. A man with keys has authority. A man with keys can open, and close, or lock up. A man with keys can operate. This is certainly not an exhaustive list. You can learn more because I am still learning. By using these basic ones you can begin operating in your supernatural ministry today.

1. Compassion: If you really want to perform miracles find someone who is hurting and show compassion. Find someone in need, and do everything in your power to meet that need. If they are a sick body, pray fervently, showing that you truly care for them. Real compassion will move you into action. Jesus was moved to compassion when he saw the people having no shepherd. He saw them hungry and He had compassion, meeting that need by the miraculous multiplication of the food. Jesus had compassion on the leper and touched him. As the widow of Nain was burying her only son, He showed compassion immediately by touching the coffin and the boy was raised back to life. Because he was filled with compassion, Jesus wept over Jerusalem. When was the last time you wept over your city? Jesus was moved with compassion throughout His ministry. It was compassion for us that held Him on the cross. If you want to be a miracle worker, get your mind off of your own problems and focus on the needs of hurting humanity. Have compassion and God will use you in miracles. Signs and wonders will follow you. Compassion makes you pull on God's power. You pull out of heaven and bring it to earth.

2. Know Who you are in Christ: This is my top priority of this book. I truly believe it is the greatest revelation that you can ever receive. Because I grew up in a very Pentecostal home, we went to church every time the doors were opened. However, I never heard how great we were in Christ. I heard how sorry I was, so I came away with a sin conscience. I did not know that I was the righteousness of God. I had no idea that I had already been accepted in the Beloved. I certainly did not know that I have been justified or I was called to be like Jesus. I thought it was heresy to even want to be like Him. Because I really didn't believe God was a good God I thought He was angry all the time. I believed that He was coming to pour His wrath out on us because he was fed up with sin. I simply did not know who I was in Christ. GO back and read Paul's revelation of what took place on Calvary. When you realize your true identity, then you will begin to operate as a son of God, anointed by His Spirit to do the impossible. I can do all things through Christ which strengthens me. WOW!

3. Know you have something to be released: After learning who you are in Christ, you will begin to learn that you have something to be released. Your faith will rise and you will begin to attempt miracles. I like what Peter said *(Acts 3)* when the first apostolic miracle took place. He told the cripple man, "LOOK ON US, silver and gold have I none but such that I have I give unto you." Freely we have received, freely we give away. We also need to be able to tell the world, "Look on us. We have your answer and His name is Jesus!" You have something to be released to the world. You have power inside of you, much like a power plant ready to ignite, and sending light into the darkness.

Ephesians 3:20, Now unto Him that is able to do exceedingly abundantly above all that we ask or think, according to the power that works in us.

Remember, it is Christ in you the hope of glory. If Christ is in you, then you definitely have the power to be released. Christ means Anointed One. It is the anointing that destroys the yoke of bondage whatever that yoke is, enabling you to minister in awesome power.

4. Be led by the Spirit: Jesus was led by the Spirit. On this note, however, everything that Jesus did, He did as a man. He operated as a man, filled and led by the Spirit. We are to exemplify the same lifestyle.

Romans 8:14, For as many as are led by the Spirit of God, they are the sons of God.

The whole earth is groaning with anticipation for the sons of God to appear *(Romans 8:19-21)*. You are what the world is waiting on.

They are hoping to encounter someone that knows Jesus. Be led by His Spirit. When I minister, I try to be very sensitive to the leading of the Spirit. I do not minister as others may do when it is time to pray for the sick or minister. Jesus did not always minister the same way, either. What matters most are results and if we are led by the Holy Spirit then we will be fruitful. I take it as a compliment when people tell me that I am different. You are unique also. So learn to depend on the Holy Spirit's guidance.

5. Prayer: *James 5:13-18, Is any among you afflicted? Let him pray. Is any merry? Let him sing psalms. Is any sick among you? Let him call for the elders of the church; and let them pray over him, anointing him with oil in the name of the Lord: And the prayer of faith shall save the sick, and the Lord shall raise him up; and if he hath committed sins, they shall be forgiven him. Confess your faults one to another, and pray one for another, that you may be healed. The effectual fervent prayer of a righteous man avails much. Elijah was a man subject to like passion as we are, and he prayed earnestly that it might not rain: and it rained not on the earth by the space of three years and six months. And he prayed again, and the heaven gave the rain, and the earth brought forth her fruit.*

I love this story because it illustrates the power of Prayer. Elijah (not Jesus), a man that the Bible states emphatically is like you and me, prayed earnestly, and he shut up the heavens with his prayers. When he prayed again the heavens gave the rain and the earth brought forth her fruit. This is a man with keys. Elijah was under the old covenant and this man still had power with God. We are under a new and better covenant. This new covenant is not in any way inferior to the old covenant. When we pray, heaven will still give up the rain, and produce more fruit on the earth. Heaven and earth continues working together. There is still power in prayer. Jesus prayed, the early apostles prayed, so we ought to pray, also. We have not because we ask not *(James 4:2)*. Ask and it shall be given, seek and you shall find, knock and it shall be opened to you *(Matthew 7:7)*. Heaven and earth are working together when we pray.

6. Declaring Dominion: We have to learn to talk right. The words of our mouth are powerful. Life and death is in the power of your tongue *(Proverbs 18:21)*. Job says to "decree a thing and it shall be established *(Job 22:28)*." Kings and rulers make decrees. Paul also said that we need to desire to prophesy *(1 Corinthians 14:1)*. Jesus taught that we can have what we say, if we only believe *(Mark 11:23)*. Sons and daughters shall prophesy *(Acts 2:17)*. When we speak the word, God is alert over His word to perform *(Jeremiah 1:12)*. Isaiah promises that God's word will never return void *(Isaiah 55:11)*. Jesus also said that the words that He speaks are spirit and life. If we are to be like Jesus, then our words should be spirit and they are filled with life. If I tell one of my sons to relay to the other one to do something, then he does it. My words did not lose any power by going through a son. Our Father's words do not lose any power just because it also goes through a son. The Bible tells us that if any man speaks, let him speak as the oracles of God *(1 Peter 4:11)*. According to your faith, prophesy! *(Romans 12:6)*

7. Giving: We are no more like God than when we give. For God so loved the world, that He gave. Jesus lived a lifestyle of a giver. He gave Himself for us. Mother Teresa has always been one of my heroes. She gave everything to serve the people of India and other parts of the world. The early church gave houses and lands. A true Christian should be a giver naturally. God has promised to bless the giver. Jesus said "Give and it shall be given unto you *(Luke 6:38)*." If you want to be a miracle worker, become a giver. God will take your little, multiply it, and do great exploits with what you gave. There is a song that has "I give myself away" in the lyrics. I love it. I want to completely give myself away. Become a giver and be like God. To live godly or even show godliness does not mean that you avoid being seen in clubs or other places. It means being like God. God is a giver!

There are many more principles, but I will stop with these. Being in covenant, or having a covenant-heart, is very important just as faith, mercy, and love are, too. Learning how the Lord speaks to you is also vital. Listening to His voice and act upon what He says. Please see my first book "Hear from Heaven and Change Your World."

You have power to be released. Daniel tells us that the people that know their God shall be strong and do exploits. Peter said, "Grace and peace be multiplied to us by the knowledge of God, and of Jesus our Lord *(2 Peter1:2)*." There are many other examples that show knowledge or KNOWING the Lord, is also a principle. We perish for lack of knowledge. We as disciples of the Lord are constantly in school - the School of the Spirit. It also continues in 2 Peter to say that by the precious promises of God we are made partakers of the DIVINE NATURE. We should desire to study His Word so that we can become more like Him and share these promises to others.

Oh, brothers and sisters, it is ministration, it is operation, it is manifestation! Those are three of the leading principles of the baptism with the Holy Ghost. And we must see to it that God is producing these three through us. The Bible is the Word of God. It has the truths, and whatever people may say of them, they stand stationary, unmovable. Not one jot or tittle shall fail of all His good promises. His Word will come forth. In heaven it is settled; on earth it must be made manifest that He is the God of everlasting power.
– Smith Wigglesworth

He that is for you is a million times more than all that can be against you… What an advantage it would be if we could only come to a place where we know that everything is within reach of us.
– Smith Wigglesworth

Chapter Ten
ICE CREAM IS A SURE THING

In this chapter, I want to briefly list a few of the precious promises that are in the Word of God. I have a small book with 199 promises, but I believe there are hundreds, if not thousands, of promises in the Word of God that we can lay hold on for ourselves. These promises will enhance our lives. They will make us more like our Lord, Jesus Christ if we can hold on to them and believe. God is not a man that He can lie. His promises are yes and amen in Him. My youngest son, Adam, learned early in life that if I promised something, then it would come to pass. I try very hard to be a man of my word, and Adam trusted me. If he wanted some ice cream, he would ask me to take him to the local Dairy Queen and get an ice cream. If I were busy, I might say that I would do it later. He would not stop asking until I said I promised. He knew that if I promised, it would be as good as having it. That is faith. God is not a man that can or will lie. His promises are sure. The Old Testament promises are mainly based on us and are conditional. For example all the blessings in the first part of Deuteronomy 28 are conditional "if we listen and we obey." They are based on our performance. The New Covenant promises are not based on works, though, lest any man should boast. They are yes, and in Him (Christ) amen. You can bank on them. They are assured mixed with faith. Faith is the currency of heaven. Your blessings are located in heavenly places in Christ *(Ephesians 1:3)*. All you have to do is be like my son Adam and simply believe the promise.

2 Peter 1:2-4, Grace and peace be multiplied unto you through the knowledge of God, and of Jesus our Lord. According as His divine power hath given unto us all things that pertains to life and godliness, through the knowledge of Him that hath called us to glory and virtue; Whereby are given unto us exceeding great and precious promises; that by these (promises) YOU might be partakers of the divine nature...

The promises are described in verse four as exceeding great and precious. The word "exceeding" means to go beyond, across, or above. It refers to being superior. If you exceed the speed limit, it means that you went beyond or above what the law allows. These promises have gone far above and beyond anything the law (Old Testament) would allow. We have a new and better covenant, with exceedingly great and precious promises.The word precious means valuable or honorable. If we had to buy these promises, none of us would have enough wealth to purchase them because they are so highly valuable. It is by these promises that we become partakers or take part in the DIVINE NATURE that is the nature of God. With these promises, we will no longer battle the nature of the old man, but we will put on the divine nature. We have been made a little lower than God Himself. This is a reference of who you really are. These promises are of extreme value. In fact, they are priceless. Remember, God sees the end from the beginning so He sees you as a mature son of His ruling and reigning with Christ. He made us in His image and in His likeness. We need to hold on to this foundation and not let go of these wonderful promises so we can be changed from glory to glory. These promises are not just for preachers or super spiritual people. They are for all of us! I am going to list a few of these promises and their scripture reference that pertain to your life. These are for your life here and now with Jesus – no matter what the circumstances are. This is not an exhaustive list. Study the Word and find others on your own!

- Promise of Eternal Life: *John 3:14-16, 1 John 2:25*
- Promise of Long Life: *Psalms 91:16, 1Ki.3:14, Pr.10:27,1Pe 3:10*
- Promise of an Abundant Life or Full Life: *Jn. 10:10*
- Promise of a Healthy Life: *3 Jn.2; De.7:15; Je.30:17*
- Promise of a Prosperous Life: *3 Jn.2; Lu.6:38; 2 Co.9:7-15*
- Promise of a Forgiven Life: *1 Jn.1:7-9; Ps. 103:3; Acts 13:38*
- Promise of a Joyful Life: *Ps.30:5; Jn. 15:11; Jn. 16:24*
- Promise of Peace: *Jn. 14:27; Jn. 16:33; Ph. 4:7*
- Promise of a Free Life: *Ps.34: 19; Jn.8:36; Ro.8:2*
- Promise of not having a Lonely Life: *Is.43:2; Mt.28:20; Mt.18:20*
- Promise of a Triumphant Life: *Ro.8:28; Ro5:17; 1Co15:57*
- Promise of a Powerful Life: *Acts1:8; Jn14:12; Ep 3:20*
- Promise of a Growing/Ever Learning Life: *Jn12:46; Jn14:26*
- Promise of a Satisfied Life: *Jn6:35; Ps23:1-6*
- Promise of a Grace Given Life: *2Co.12:9; Ep4:7; 2Pe1:2-4*
- Promise of Provision: *Ph4:19; Ps31:19; Mt6:33*
- Promise of a Supernatural Life: *Ph4:13; Mk9:23*

There are many more promises with many more scripture that relate to the above promises. 2 Timothy 2:15 commands us to "Study to show thyself approved unto God, a workman that needs not to be ashamed, rightly dividing the word of Truth." Many people think these promises apply only after we pass from this life, but we really do not pass. Eternal Life starts the day you receive Jesus as your

Lord and Savior. These promises and all the other ones will help you enjoy life to the fullest extent. By applying these promises you can take part in the divine nature. Remember, a promise is only as good as the one doing the promising. Since God, our Father, cannot lie, He cannot fail. Everything that He has spoken shall surely come to pass. If my promise was good enough for my son Adam to believe for his ice cream, then how much more should we believe in the promises of our heavenly Father?

1 Kings 8:56, Blessed be the Lord, that hath given rest unto His people Israel, according to all that He hath promised: there hath not failed one word of all His good promise, which He promised...

Romans 4:21, And being fully persuaded, that what he had promised, he was able also to perform.

Hebrews 11:6, But without faith it is impossible to please Him; for he that cometh to God must believe that He is (able, good, willing), and that He is a rewarder of them that diligently seek Him.

I believe that our Father in heaven would rather have us question His ability than question His willingness. We all know that He is able to do anything, but we are not sure He is willing. God is willing to help us in our times of trouble. He has already given His Son. Everything else is secondary. Jesus has paid the full price for our full salvation. Salvation, or being saved, comes from the Greek word "sozo." Sozo means to be rescued, delivered, saved, prospered, and made whole. It implies healings, salvation, prosperity, and every other blessing

THE REAL MAN IN THE MIRROR

that enhances our ability to live the abundant life that Jesus said He came to give us *(John 10:10)*.

I will conclude in the following pages with reminders of who you are in Christ. There will be plenty of scripture reference so that you can study and meditate on them. Let God speak to you. Faith comes by hearing (not having heard), and hearing by the Word of God. If you were raised like I was, some of you may have objections that will come to your mind. While studying these, let God be true and submit to the Word of God. Bow your knee to the truth. A false sense of humility will not help you in any way. Pride also goes before destruction. True humility is receiving all that God has for you and knowing you had absolutely nothing to do with earning it. It is all unmerited. It is only by grace, which should cause us to lift our hands and hearts in adoration and praise. Paul said, "I should somewhat more boast of my authority." Can you speak openly about what is true of you? When you come into agreement with God, your effectiveness will show what God says about you is truer than anything anyone else can possibly say about you. Start living the resurrected life today. Eternity started when you received the Lord, Jesus Christ, into your life. Let Him walk in your temple as King of kings and Lord of lords.

The Bible is the Word of God: supernatural in origin, eternal in duration, inexpressible in valor, infinite in scope, regenerative in power, infallible in authority, universal in interest, personal in application, inspired in totality. Read it through, write it down, pray it in, work it out, and then pass it on. Truly the Word of God changes a man until he becomes an "epistle of God." It transform his mind, changes his character, moves him from grace to grace, and makes him an inheritor of the very nature of God, God comes in, dwells in, walks in, talks through, and sups with him who opens his being to the Word of God.

– Smith Wigglesworth

Century after century – there it stands. Empires rise and fall and are forgotten – there it stands. Dynasty succeeds dynasty – there it stands. Emperors decree its extermination – there it stands. Atheists rail against it – there it stands. Agnostics smile cynically – there it stands. Profane, prayerless, punsters exaggerate its meaning – there it stands. Unbelief abandons it – there it stands. The tooth of time gnaws but makes no dent in it – there it stands. Infidels predict its abandonment – there it stands. Modernism tries to explain it away – there it stands.

– A.Z. Conrad

Chapter Eleven

CONCLUSION: WHO ARE YOU, REALLY?

Philemon 6, That the communication of thy faith may become effectual by the acknowledging of every good thing which is in you in Christ Jesus.

According to this verse, before I can communicate the gospel effectively, I must acknowledge every good thing which is in me. I was taught not to brag about myself. This was difficult for me to put into practice but after I started focusing on my good qualities, I began to mature really fast. God started opening up doors for me like never before. Remember, anything good in me is because of Jesus. We are dead! So I started acknowledging the wisdom of God, the power of God, and the anointing of God. I began to acknowledge all the good characteristics in me. Really! I began to acknowledge Jesus in all of His glory. This is who that is in you. He is the real man in the mirror. I want to leave you with the following verse that Paul left the Ephesians after a ministry trip there.

Acts 20:32, And now, brethren, I commend you to God, and to the word of His grace, which is able to build you up, and to give you an inheritance among all them which are sanctified.

These scriptures on the next few pages portray your true identity. They are filled with grace, meant to encourage and remind you of your inheritance. The Word has power. Prepare your heart to receive the Word.

Who You Are in Christ?
You are a New Creation: *2 Co 5:17*
You are justified: *Ro 5:1*
You are Complete in Christ: *Colossians 2:10*
You are a Saint: *Ep. 1:1*
You are the elect: *Ro. 8:33*
You are His Workmanship (Masterpiece): *Ep.2:10*
You are hid in God: *Col.3:3*
You are a king: *Rev1:5-6*
You are a priest: *Rev1:6*
You are a chosen generation: *1Peter2:9*
You are a royal priesthood: *1Peter2:9*
You are a holy nation: *1 Peter2:9*
You are a peculiar people: *1Peter2:9*
You are Holy, Sanctified, and Perfected: *Hebrews10:9-14*
You are an able minister: *2Co3:6*
You are a living epistle: *2Co3:2*
You are a lively stone: *1Peter2:5*
You are a spiritual house: *1Peter2:5*
You are a holy priesthood *1Peter2:5*
You are free from condemnation: *Ro.8:1-2*
You are free period (in all things): *Jo.8:32, 36; 2Co.3:17*
You are united with the Lord: *1Co.6:17*
You are a minister of reconciliation: *2Co.5:17-19*
You are an ambassador: 2Co.5:17-20
You are the righteousness of God: *2Co.5:17-21*

You are assured that all things work together for our good: *Ro.8:28*
You are bought with a price and now belong to God: *1Co.6:19-20*
You are God's temple: *1Co.3:16*
You can do all things: *Ph4:13*
You are established, anointed, & sealed by God: *2Co.1:21-22*
You are seated with Christ: *Ep2:6*
You are a member of Christ's body: *1 Co12:27*
You are a son of God: *Jn1:12; Ga4:1; Ro8*
You are God's co-laborer or fellow worker: *1Co3:9*
You are a branch of the True Vine and a fruit producer: *Jn 15;1-8*
You have been chosen and appointed to bear fruit: *Jn15:16*
You are His disciples: *Mt28:18-20*
You are the salt of the earth: *Mt5:13-14*
You are the light of the world: *Mt5:13-14*
You are a witness of the Lord Jesus: *Acts1:8*
You are a citizen of Heaven: *Ph3:20*
You have a spirit of power, love, and sound mind: *2Tim1:7*
You have been redeemed and forgiven: *Co 1:14*
You are free from any charges against you: *Ro8:33-34*
You are an heir of God and joint heir with Christ Jesus: *Ro 8:15-17*
You are a son led by the Holy Spirit: *Ro 8:14*
You are more than a Conqueror: *Ro8:37*
You are inseparable from the Love of God: *Ro8:38-39*
You are free to approach God at any time: *Ep3:11-12; He4:16*
You may find grace and mercy in time of need: *He4:16*
You are assured that what God starts, He will complete: *Ph1:6*
You are a friend of Christ: *Jn15:15*
You are a brother of Christ: *Ro8:29*
You are filled with all joy and peace: *Ro15:13*

You are healed: *Is53:3-5*
You are accepted in the Beloved: *Ep1:6*
You are rich: *1Co3:21; 1Co4:8; 2Co8:9*
You are blessed with every spiritual blessing: *Ep.1:3*

We will stop with Ep1:3 because this verse summarizes it all to me. We are in Christ and there we have all blessings. This is definitely not an exhaustive list, but it is enough to get you started to transforming your mind to becoming more like Christ. The more you reaffirm your true identity, focusing on who you are in Christ, the more your behavior will begin to reflect that identity. You are so beautiful to God. You are perfect! Philemon 6 tells us to acknowledge every good thing in you. Start today! The world needs to see Jesus, and they can see Him through you.

To be like Jesus is your destiny. Jesus is the real man in the mirror. God bless you as you fulfill your purpose and reach your destiny. God has great plans for you and desires to use you to change the world. If the devil had known the plans that God had for you, he would have never crucified Jesus. Instead of Jesus walking around in one location, now there are millions of Christians ministering all over the world. Can you imagine what would happen if we would all get a revelation of our full potential in Christ? It would be glorious! It would be the manifestation of Jesus all over the world. It is now happening in believers from all corners of the globe and from every tribe and tongue. Will you allow Jesus to come in His fullness in your life, too? Will you exemplify this life of His by revealing the glory that is in you right now? You already have it. So now begin manifesting the love, the wisdom, and the power of the King and

His kingdom. Lord Jesus, Thy Kingdom Come, Thy Will be done as it is in Heaven so let it be in earth. Come Lord Jesus, come quickly.

Far too many of us dwell on the lowlands of salvation. Can't you hear voices calling you up to the uplands of divine grace? Mountain climbing is thrilling! Let's be off! Hebron's heights rise before us. Shall we explore our unclaimed inheritance in the heavenlies?
– Smith Wigglesworth

I can get more out of God by believing Him for one minute than by shouting at Him all night
– Smith Wigglesworth

We pass out of the Old creation and into the New through the Inbreathed Breath of God.
– Derek Prince

NOTES

1. An Encyclopedia of Compelling Quotations by Daniel Watkins
2. Ephesians, Life Application Bible Commentary
3. Aion, The Eternal Vision, The Ultimate Collections of Spiritual Quotations compiled by William Sykes

Introduction
4. The Anointing of His Spirit: Showing Forth His Glory
5. Lord, What Do You Want Me To Do? The Wigglesworth Standard, P.J. Madden
6. An Encyclopedia of Compelling Quotations by Daniel Watkins

Chapter 1
Beautiful One
7. The Ordinary Made Extraordinary, The Anointing of His Spirit
8. Count It All Joy, The Anointing of the Spirit, Smith Wigglessworth

Chapter 2
You Look Better Than You Think
9. God's Treasure House, The Anointing of His Spirit by Smith Wigglesworth
10. The Reality, Advanced Bible Course, Studies in the Deeper Life, E.W. Kenyon

Chapter 3
You Are Not Common
11. Flames of Fire, The Wigglesworth Standard, P.J. Madden
12. Lord, What Do You Want Me To Do? The Wigglesworth Standard by P.J. Madden
13. Christ For The Nations, Inc. book, edited by Gordon Lindsay, pg 83-84

Chapter 4
Jesus Comes To His Temple
14. The Hidden Man of the Heart, Advanced Bible Course, Studies in the Deeper Life

Chapter 5
Lessons From The Wise Master Builder
15. Dominion, Adventures In God by John G. Lake
16. The Hidden Man Of The Heart, Advanced Bible Course, Studies In The Deeper Life, E.W. Kenyon
17. The Tangibility Of The Spirit, The John G. Lake Sermons on Dominion Over Demons, Disease, and Death
18. An Encyclopedia of Compelling Quotations by Daniel Watkins

Chapter 6
Jesus Is With Us
19. What The Church Has Failed To See, Advanced Bible Course, Studies In The Deeper Life
20. Ephesians, The Christ In The Bible Commentary, Volume 5

Chapter 7
Paul's Revelation
21. Receiving Power From On High, The Anointing Of His Spirit
22. Ephesians, Life Application Bible Commentary
23. Remark to John Hancock at the signing of the Declaration of Independence, 4 July 1776, pg 741, An Encyclopedia of Compelling Quotations, R. Daniel Watkins

Chapter 8
The New Wine Is In The Cluster
24. Holy Bible, King James Version, John 15:5
25. Dominion, Adventures In God by John G. Lake
26. Mighty Manifestations by Reinhard Bonnke

Chapter 9
Power Releasing Principles
27. Showing Forth His Glory, The Anointing Of His Spirit by Smith Wigglesworth
28. The Wigglesworth Standard by P.J. Madden

Chapter 10
Ice Cream Is A Sure Thing
29. The Wigglesworth Standard by P.J. Madden
30. Hear From HEaven, Dale Carver, Creation House Press, pg. 45-46
31. www.thegoodnessofgod.com / Wigglesworth quotes
32. www.worldofquotes.com, famous quotes by Smith Wigglesworth
33. The Holy Spirit In You by Derek Prince

Other titles by Dr. Dale Carver

For more information about the ministry of Dr. Dale Carver,
to request a speaking engagement, or to purchase additional
copies of this book or the titles referenced above,
please contact:

GRAB The World Ministries
Dr. Dale Carver
Founder/President

1497 West 12th Street
Alma, Georgia 31510

912-632-3744
adcarver@bellsouth.net

CPSIA information can be obtained at www.ICGtesting.com
Printed in the USA
LVOW060725170313

324460LV00003BA/9/P